TEACHER'S MANUAL WITH ANSWERS

Thirteen Steps to Better Writing

Joan D. Berbrich, Ph.D.

AMSCO SCHOOL PUBLICATIONS, INC.
315 Hudson Street / New York, N.Y. 10013

When ordering this book, please specify
either **R 437 T** or THIRTEEN STEPS TO BETTER
WRITING TEACHER'S MANUAL.

ISBN 0-87720-667-8

Printed in the United States of America

CONTENTS

INTRODUCTION
    Contents of the Text   *1*
    Using the Text   *2*
    Contents of the Teacher's Manual   *3*

UNIT ONE
    STEP I.   **USE SPECIFIC NOUNS**
        1. Specific Nouns: Learn Them!   *8*
        2. Specific Nouns: Use Them!   *13*
        3. Specific Nouns: Use Them in *Your* Writing!   *15*
    STEP II.   **USE SPECIFIC VERBS**
        4. Specific Verbs: Learn Them!   *17*
        5. Specific Verbs: Use Them!   *19*
        6. Specific Verbs: Use Them in *Your* Writing!   *21*
    STEP III.   **USE APT ADJECTIVES**
        7. Apt Adjectives: Learn Them!   *23*
        8. Apt Adjectives: Use Them!   *28*
        9. Apt Adjectives: Use Them in *Your* Writing!   *29*
    WRITING TIME—I   *31*
    PREPARATION FOR UNIT TEST ONE   *33*

UNIT TWO
    STEP IV.   **USE AGILE ADVERBS**
        10. Agile Adverbs: Learn Them!   *35*
        11. Agile Adverbs: Use Them!   *37*

          12. Agile Adverbs: Use Them in *Your*
              Writing!   *39*

STEP V.   **USE PERSONAL PRONOUNS CORRECTLY**
          13. Personal Pronouns: Learn Them!   *42*
          14. Personal Pronouns: Use Them!   *43*
          15. Personal Pronouns: Use Them in *Your*
              Writing!   *47*

STEP VI.   **USE PURPOSEFUL PREPOSITIONS**
          16. Purposeful Prepositions: Learn Them!   *49*
          17. Purposeful Prepositions: Use Them!   *53*
          18. Purposeful Prepositions: Use Them in
              Your Writing!   *55*

WRITING TIME—II   *57*
PREPARATION FOR UNIT TEST TWO   *59*

UNIT THREE
STEP VII.   **USE ALL FOUR TYPES OF SENTENCES**
          19. Four Types of Sentences: Learn Them!   *61*
          20. Four Types of Sentences: Use Them!   *62*
          21. Four Types of Sentences: Use Them in
              Your Writing!   *65*

STEP VIII.   **USE COMPOUND SENTENCES**
          22. Compound Sentences: Learn Them!   *67*
          23. Compound Sentences: Use Them!   *69*
          24. Compound Sentences: Use Them in
              Your Writing!   *71*

STEP IX.   **USE COMPLEX SENTENCES**
          25. Complex Sentences: Learn Them!   *73*
          26. Complex Sentences: Use Them!   *76*
          27. Complex Sentences: Use Them in *Your*
              Writing!   *79*

WRITING TIME—III   *82*
PREPARATION FOR UNIT TEST THREE   *83*

UNIT FOUR

STEP X.   USE APPOSITIVES

28. Appositives: Learn Them!   *85*

29. Appositives: Use Them!   *87*

30. Appositives: Use Them in *Your* Writing!   *90*

STEP XI.   USE PARALLEL STRUCTURE

31. Parallel Structure: Learn It!   *93*

32. Parallel Structure: Use It!   *96*

33. Parallel Structure: Use It in *Your* Writing!   *98*

STEP XII.   USE VERBALS

34. Verbals: Learn Them!   *100*

35. Verbals: Use Them!   *104*

36. Verbals: Use Them in *Your* Writing!   *107*

STEP XIII.   USE SENTENCE COMBINING

37. Combining Sentences: Nursery Level   *109*

38. Combining Sentences: Junior Level   *112*

39. Combining Sentences: Senior Level   *114*

40. Combining Sentences: Use Them in *Your* Writing!   *118*

WRITING TIME—IV   *118*

PREPARATION FOR UNIT TEST FOUR   *119*

PORTFOLIO I. SNAKES   *121*

1. Finding Answers   *121*

2. Writing a Report   *122*

3. Writing a Friendly Letter   *122*

4. Writing a Fable   *123*

PORTFOLIO II. NAMES   *124*

5. Writing a Filler   *124*

6. Writing a Book   *124*

7. Writing a Friendly Letter   *125*

8. Writing a Report   *125*

PORTFOLIO III. MOVIES   *126*

9. Writing a Business Letter   *126*

10. Writing a Report   *126*
11. Writing a Persuasive Letter   *126*

ANSWERS: UNIT TEST ONE   *129*
ANSWERS: UNIT TEST TWO   *130*
ANSWERS: UNIT TEST THREE   *132*
ANSWERS: UNIT TEST FOUR   *134*

INTRODUCTION

Thirteen Steps to Better Writing? Why thirteen? Why not six? Or eighteen? Or—for that matter—why not one hundred one?

Thirteen is an arbitrary number, but a reasonable one, too. It is the number of writing skills a student might be expected to learn, to master, *and* to apply in one year.

Contents of the Text

The thirteen techniques (or steps) include the handling of:

Parts of Speech

I. Specific Nouns
II. Specific Verbs
III. Apt Adjectives
IV. Agile Adverbs
V. Personal Pronouns
VI. Purposeful Prepositions

PLUS

Various Kinds of Sentences

VII. The Four Types of Sentences: Declarative, Interrogative, Imperative, and Exclamatory
VIII. The Compound Sentence (including the coordinate conjunction)
IX. The Complex Sentence (including the subordinate conjunction)

1

Variations in Sentence Structure

    X.   Appositives
    XI.   Parallel Structure
    XII.   Verbals (infinitives, participles, and gerunds)
    XIII.   Combining Sentences

The twelfth technique—the use of verbals—might logically be included in the first section; but since most students find verbals difficult, it has been placed in the latter part of the text.

PLUS

Writing Time—Special units that follow Steps III, VI, IX, and XIII. These review the material learned in the preceding chapters through work in revision and in original writing.

PLUS

Three Portfolios—Each of these deals with material of interest to students (snakes, names, and movie special effects). Each requires the application of all the techniques in the writing of reports and of both friendly and business letters.

Using the Text

Why are specific techniques taught separately? Aren't they all related?

Of course. And some people (a rare few) learn to write as they learned to talk—by a kind of osmosis. Most of us, though, learn to write step by step, the way we learn to cook, or repair a car, or cultivate a garden.

Will a mastery of the "Thirteen Steps" guarantee that a student will be a good writer?

No. But it will guarantee that a student will be a *better* writer than he or she was before. Not everyone can write truly well; but almost every-

2

one can write competently. Besides—to write like Shakespeare, a student would have to master dozens of esoteric techniques like antithesis and paradox, oxymoron and personification, and have a touch of genius!

How long should it take students to work their way through this text in its entirety?

If students work with this text two periods a week, they should complete it in a year. If students work with this text five periods a week, they should complete it in twelve to fifteen weeks.

We recommend the first approach. Spaced over a year with frequent repetition and time for assimilation, these techniques—or most of them—should become almost automatic and therefore should become part of a student's permanent repertoire of writing skills.

How you use this text is for *you* to decide. Only you know the students in your classes. Only you know what they need and how best they learn. To help you and to increase the usefulness of this text is the twofold purpose of this manual. It is the reason for the varied procedures and for the large variety of follow-up exercises. We hope it helps you to engage your students in enjoyable and valuable experiences in the world of writing.

Contents of the Teacher's Manual

As you know, each class is different from every other class. Each *group* of students becomes a kind of entity that requires special treatment and motivation. What works beautifully in one class may not work in another. What challenges one class may frustrate another. What amuses and grips one class may totally bore another. So the main purpose of this manual is to provide dozens of approaches that will enable you to adapt this text for various classes and even for various individual students.

1. **Preparation.** Most of the "Thirteen Steps" begin with a preparation exercise to review what your students already know and to offer new material in a challenging way. The student who understands the meaning of the word "compound" will find it easier to

3

understand (and remember) what a compound sentence is. The student who has searched his or her memory for ads using appositives will know what an appositive is—even before learning the definition. Preparation of this type is helpful to all students but is essential for the less able ones.

2. **Varied Approaches.** As you know, the same lesson can be taught in a dozen different ways. Varied approaches are listed so that you can "pick and choose" selecting, for example, a method that will work with your fifth period class on the day before a vacation. At times specific approaches are suggested for less able students, at other times for gifted students. Occasionally, small-group work is recommended, both as a change of pace and as an opportunity to "brainstorm" and to share ideas.

3. **Vocabulary.** Vocabulary in this manual is handled in three different ways:

    (a) *Technical Vocabulary.* This includes the definitions of a noun, an infinitive, a complex sentence, etc. If students understand these terms clearly, communication in the classroom should be more effective and correction should be easier because you are able to offer concrete suggestions for revision.

    (b) *Tangential Vocabulary.* These are interesting or unusual nouns, verbs, and adjectives in addition to occasional words used in the text. Students who consult a dictionary for the meaning of a word, who examine the word in context, and who use it in their own writing, are on their way to improving their permanent vocabularies.

    (c) *Word Origins.* Exciting or provocative word origins add interest to the students' writing. Students who know the origin of many words in daily usage gain new insight into language and new appreciation for words and their connotations.

4. **Practice.** Repetition is essential if permanent learning is to take place. Therefore, many opportunities for additional practice are provided. How many you use depends, of course, on you and on a particular class's needs.

5. **Media.** Newspapers, magazines, radio, and television play a major role in the dissemination of information in this country. During their adult lives, students will constantly be both receiving and evaluating material communicated through the media. Many suggested optional activities send students to one or more of the media both to apply new knowledge and to evaluate.

6. **Research.** While in-depth research is beyond the ability of most young students, even they can profit from a knowledge of the library and from an occasional experience in finding and organizing material. For this reason, activities are suggested that encourage the students to do some research about folklore, unusual local celebrations, interesting facts and outstanding speeches. One activity even takes students into the acquiring and use of oral history.

7. **Special Writing.** In addition to the writing exercises of various lengths and types, special activities are described that enable students to collect individual pieces of writing and "publish" them as a class booklet. Some examples: a booklet of unusual celebrations throughout the United States, a booklet of class names and their origins, a booklet analyzing unusually successful movies and TV programs. These booklets provide the students with opportunities to share their writing with others.

8. **Games.** Grammar can be boring, especially in the initial stages of learning and in the necessary drill. For this reason games have been provided that will amuse, challenge, and reinforce learning. Young people seem to be naturally competitive and will work harder to recognize adverbs or provide specific nouns if they are competing with one another. The use of games is especially recommended for review, for the last five or ten minutes of a period, and on the day preceding a vacation or holiday. Through games, time that is normally "lost" can be used—and used effectively.

9. **Miscellaneous.** Scattered throughout the manual are additional exercises dealing with alliteration, puns, repetition, alphabetizing, spelling, point of view and punctuation. Some of these you may wish to use with one class only (or with one student); others you may find helpful for all your classes. As always, the choice is yours.

These optional activities give you, the teacher, the widest possible latitude—the freedom to pick and choose the kinds of exercises needed by your students. It should help you to use the same material and the same text in several classes but with varied approaches and methods so that your lesson plans for each class will be truly "custom-made."

10. **Unit Tests.** The Unit Tests are published in a separate booklet. When ordering the test booklet ask for R 438 U or *Unit Tests for Thirteen Steps to Better Writing*. At the end of each section (Steps I–III, IV–VI, VII–IX, and X–XIII) a two-part test is given. The first part tests the student's memory by asking questions that can be answered only if the student has successfully completed the unit. The second part tests the student's ability to *apply* the skills learned in the section to new material. The two parts can be administered as one test, or either part can be used independently. The early unit tests have deliberately been made fairly easy so that students can feel a sense of accomplishment and can be motivated to continue work.

11. **Answers.** Answers to the questions in the text are given in this manual along with suggested teaching procedures. In most cases, these are suggested answers. There is seldom only *one* correct answer. Answers to the Unit Tests appear at the end of this manual. Different students will create different sentences and paragraphs in different ways, based on their own experiences and attitudes. Certainly it is this variation that makes the teaching of English such a complex and difficult task—and such a joy!

One Last Note

There are few things we enjoy doing in a vacuum. If we cook, we take pleasure in watching others devour the results of our cooking. If we speak, we watch intently to see if others are listening and truly hearing. And if we write, we want to know that others are reading and reacting to our writing. As far as you can, give your students opportunities to write for a specific purpose, and for particular readers. Encourage them to write "Letters to the Editor" and to submit them to school and local newspapers. Encourage them to write friendly letters to relatives

6

and friends—and to experience the joy of receiving answers. Encourage them to place booklets of their writing in the school library so that they will see other students reading (and perhaps chuckling at) what they have written. Encourage them to read one another's writing and to comment on it. Encourage them to take home pieces of writing they are especially proud of, and to bask in the interest and admiration of parents and siblings. Encourage them to write sometimes just for *you*. In turn, encourage the students by writing your own comments on their papers. (On the basis of 1 to 10: a grade counts 5 as a motivating factor; a humorous or admiring comment counts 10!)

UNIT ONE

Invite the students to open their books to page 2. Introduce the First Step to Better Writing—Specific Nouns. Explain that mastery of this first step will help them to become better writers, and it will also help them to think and speak more clearly.

Call the students' attention to the display box and point out the differences in the two sentences.

STEP I, Chapter 1, Specific Nouns: Learn Them!
Pages 3–6

PREPARATION

Although most of your students will already know what a noun is, they can always profit from review. Remind them that a NOUN is the name of a person, place, or thing. Then list—or have one of the students list—on the chalkboard four groups of nouns, in each case providing the category and the first example.

	GENERAL	SPECIFIC
1.	Names of land areas:	
	continent	Europe
	country	_____
	state	_____
	city	_____
	town	_____
	village	_____
2.	Names of people:	
	man	Mr. Stein
	woman	_____

        boy   _____
        girl   _____
        child   _____

3.   Names of creatures:

        animal   ___dog_____
        bird   _____
        fish   _____
        insect   _____

4.   Names of foods:

        meat   __chicken__
        vegetable   _____
        dessert   _____
        beverage   _____
        snack   _____

Point out that these are *general* nouns that name a type of class. Now ask the students to provide a *specific* noun for each of the *general* nouns. Write the specific nouns in the second columns on the chalkboard. Some possible answers are:

1.   continent   North America
     country   U.S.A.
     state   California
     county   Orange
     city   Anaheim
     town   Lakeland
     village   Homedale

2.   man   Joe Brown
     woman   Melissa Green
     boy   Andy
     girl   Barbara
     child   Timmy

3. animal   buffalo
    bird   robin
    fish   goldfish
    insect   ant

4. meat   pork
    vegetable   spinach
    dessert   ice cream
    beverage   tea
    snack   popcorn

Point out that *general* nouns are almost always *common* nouns and are not capitalized. *Specific* nouns are sometimes *proper* nouns (groups 1 and 2) and are then capitalized; but sometimes they, too, are *common* nouns (groups 3 and 4) and are not capitalized.

A. Have students do Exercise A (page 3). Correct and discuss.

Meats: pork; turkey; lamb
Potatoes: baked; scalloped; boiled; mashed
Vegetables: peas; carrots; spinach

B. Have students do Exercise B (page 4). Correct and discuss.

1. caramels; chocolate bars; jawbreakers
2. a woolly scarf; ski pants; high boots
3. *Tom Sawyer*; *The Red Pony*; *Kon-Tiki*
4. *The Bill Cosby Show*; *Benson*; *Different Strokes*
5. bat; ball; catcher's mask

C. Have students do Exercise C (page 4). Correct and discuss.

1. (Answers will vary considerably.)
2. cottage; two-family; condominium; split-level; colonial; apartment; shack; houseboat; trailer

D. For Exercise D (page 5), there are several possible procedures.

1. You may wish to do this orally in class letting students volunteer answers.

10

2. You may assign for homework, suggesting students refer to dictionaries and any other reference books available.

This exercise is both a game and a learning experience. To make it more of a learning experience, challenge the students (or let them challenge one another) as to the meaning or description of the terms on their lists. *Suggestion:* Similar lists with different categories can form a useful lesson to have on hand for a substitute. Some possible categories: foods, colors, countries, cars, rock groups, movies and hobbies.

CLOTHING	ANIMALS	TREES	FLOWERS
anorak	aardvark	ash	aster
blouse	baboon	birch	begonia
cardigan	cat	chestnut	carnation
dirndl	dog	dogwood	daisy
earmuff	elephant	elm	edelweiss
furs	fox	fir	forget-me-not
gloves	giraffe	gingko	geranium
hood	hippopotamus	hickory	hyacinth
inverness	impala	ironwood	iris
jacket	jackal	juniper	jonquil
kimono	koala	kumquat	king cup
lingerie	lion	laurel	lily
mitten	mink	maple	marigold
necktie	narwhal	Norway spruce	nasturtium
overcoat	otter	oak	orchid
pants	panther	pine	pansy
q?	quagga	quince	Queen Anne's Lace
raincoat	rhinoceros	redwood	rose
shirt	skunk	sycamore	snapdragon
tights	tiger	tulip tree	tulip
underwear	unicorn	umbrella	u?
vest	vicuna	Virginia pine	violet
wristlet	wolf	weeping willow	wisteria
x?	x?	x?	x?
yarmulka	yak	yew	yellow jessamine
zootsuit	zebra	zebrawood	zinnia

E.   If possible, have a class set of dictionaries available for this exercise. Help students to explore the wonder of words. As they find *collywobbles* and write the meaning, talk about the word. Does the word "fit" the meaning? Is it exactly right? Does it convey the way you feel when you have an upset stomach? Do this with all five words; then have the students proceed with the exercise. Check answers, and discuss.

    1. bellyache; queasiness in stomach
    2. a bitter, usually public quarrel or fight; a free-for-all
    3. an utterly ignorant person
    4. one who boasts a great deal
    5. a sermon; a lecture
    6 and 7.   (Answers will vary considerably.)
    8. braggart
    9. homily
   10. collywobbles
   11. ignoramus
   12. donnybrook
   13 and 14.   (Answers will vary considerably.)

VARIATIONS AND FOLLOW-UPS

1. *Practice.* Ask students to look around the classroom and draw up a list of the names of *things* (not people) that they see (chalkboard, wall, ceiling, desks, books, etc.). Give them five minutes and challenge them to find as many nouns as possible. After the five minutes are up, have them count the number of nouns to see who is the *noun champion*. Have the champ read her or his list, and let others challenge any word that they doubt is a noun.

2. *Extending Their Knowledge.* This would be a good time to review subject-verb agreement. Point out that any noun can be used as the subject of a sentence, but that the subject and the verb must agree in *number* . . . that is, a singular noun must be followed by a singular verb; a plural noun by a plural verb.
    One *child is* going to Disneyland.
    Two *children are* going to Disneyland.
After you are sure the students understand the difference between

singular and plural (both for nouns and for verbs), have them write *is* or *are* after each noun in the list they drew up for Exercise 1 above. Check a few orally.

3. *Game.* Tell students the object of this game is to guess the noun that names a thing in the classroom. Then say (or have a student say): "I'm thinking of a noun that begins with 'w' and has four letters." Students volunteer answers. (WALL.) They may get noisy, but this is a good way, especially with less able students, to review spelling as well as nouns.

4. *Game.* For this game, provide the students with dictionaries (all of one type). Then say: "I'm thinking of a noun (on page _?_ of the dictionary) that means talent or an instinctive skill (FLAIR)." This works best with better students and will improve their vocabulary and dictionary skills as well as their knowledge of nouns.

STEP I, Chapter 2, Specific Nouns: Use Them!
Pages 7–11

A. Have students complete exercise. Check immediately and discuss as needed.

1. leopard
2. Jaguar
3. France, Belgium, and England
4. cornflakes . . . strawberries
5. *Family Ties*

B. Less able students may need a little help with this exercise. All others should be able to handle it easily. Check and discuss.

1. The ballerina entered the theater.
2. The doctor entered the hospital.
3. The clerk entered the store.
4. The shoplifter entered the supermarket.
5. The teller entered the bank.

C. Have students complete the exercise. Check and discuss.

    1. The leopard clawed the oak.
    2. The robin ate a fly.
    3. The weightlifter did some push-ups.
    4. The toddler threw a vase.
    5. The pianist played "The Blue Danube."

D. After students have completed this exercise, ask several of them to read their paragraphs aloud. Discuss how different people handle the same problem in different ways: from different points of view, with different vocabulary.

1.	(a)	weeping willow	5.	(h)	six feet
	(b)	cardinal		(i)	cardinal
2.	(c)	cat		(j)	St. Bernard
	(d)	cardinal	6.	(k)	cat
3.	(e)	greed		(l)	cardinal
	(f)	cat		(m)	St. Bernard's
4.	(g)	belly			

    Up in the weeping willow, a cardinal sang, its voice warm and melodious. Nearby, a cat crouched, watching the cardinal. Greed made the cat's eyes glitter. Stealthily it began to slink forward, belly to the ground. It was only six feet from the bird when a St. Bernard dashed toward it from the next yard. As the cat fled, the cardinal flew down and perched confidently on the St. Bernard's head.

VARIATIONS AND FOLLOW-UPS

1. **Extending Their Knowledge.** Did anyone set the paragraph in the tropics, using perhaps a palm tree, a cockatoo, a tiger cub, and an elephant? Point out that the writer could set this little scene any-

where: in the tropics, in the Australian Outback, in Chicago, in the Far North. But—the setting and the "characters" must be consistent. For fun (and learning too) let the students work together to set the paragraph in various locations, always changing the "characters" to suit the setting.

2. **Game.** Select ten students to participate in a "specific noun bee." Give a general noun for which each participant must provide a specific one. EXAMPLE: general noun—building; specific noun—chalet. Any student who cannot provide a specific noun sits down. The rest of the class should keep track of the specific nouns mentioned to be sure none is repeated. Some general nouns useful for this game:

buildings	school subjects	crops
states	vegetables	farming equipment
sports	fruits	board games
appliances		

    This game will work best if you suit the category to your students: e.g., farming equipment in a rural area. The game can be repeated two or three times until all students have participated, but a different category should be used with each group.

3. **Alphabetizing.** This is a variation and an extension based on Exercise 2. Ask students who are not participating to arrange in an *alphabetized* list all specific nouns mentioned. At the end of the game, ask for a volunteer to read the list aloud and check it for accuracy and for correct alphabetical order. Point out that it is possible to alphabetize quickly by putting, "a" words at the top of the page, "m" words about halfway down and "z" words near the bottom and inserting other words in approximate order.

STEP I, Chapter 3, Specific Noun: Use Them in *Your Writing*
Pages 12–15

A. Students should have little trouble with this exercise. After they have finished, have a few students read their paragraphs aloud and discuss. (Answers will vary.)

B. Same procedure as in A. (Answers will vary.)

C. Same procedure as in A. Although this exercise is complex, directions are very detailed, and students should be able to handle it with ease. (Answers will vary.)
Point out WRITING TECHNIQUE 1 at the bottom of page 15.

VARIATIONS AND FOLLOW-UPS

1. **Point of view.** After students have completed Exercise C, try this. Ask them to close their eyes for a moment and *envision* the front of the school building. Then ask them to mention (and write on the chalkboard) every object they can envision, with details. EXAMPLE: steps to front door: how many?—made of what?—how wide? After they have listed as many details as possible, ask them to indicate which ones they would use to describe the front of the building from the point of view of . . .

   (a) a would-be burglar, at night
   (b) a new student entering the building for the first time
   (c) a principal on her or his first day

   Now suggest that the students look again at their answers to Exercise C. Did they write from a particular point of view? If not, would the paragraph be better if they did? If you wish to give them additional writing practice, have them write a new paragraph (on the same topic or a different one) from a very specific point of view—using, of course, strong specific nouns. This exercise will review and reinforce their use of specific nouns and introduce them to *point of view*.

2. **Generalization to Supporting Details.** If your students need more work on this method of organization, try this: Give them a general statement, and ask them to provide supporting details. This can be done orally or in writing.
   Some possible generalizations:

   (a) A baseball team is made up of nine players.
   (b) As I entered the park, I was stunned by the battalions of beautiful flowers.

(c) Strolling into the fast-food restaurant, I noticed all kinds of people around me.

(d) Jim drove up in his car, eager to show it to us.

Then, especially with more able students, move on to more abstract generalizations:

(e) Winter is coming.

(f) In our government, elected representatives make the laws.

STEP II, Chapter 4, Specific Verbs: Learn Them!
Pages 17–21

PREPARATION

Most of your students will already know what a verb is, but they can always profit from review. Remind them that a VERB is a word that expresses action or a state of being.

Ask them to suggest action verbs—words that describe things they *do* everyday—such as EAT and WALK and WASH. List these on the chalkboard. When there are 25 or 30 words listed, have the students copy the list on a piece of scrap paper and place it to one side. (If they need work in alphabetizing, let them alphabetize the list first.)

Introduce the students to the Second Step to Better Writing—Specific Verbs. Point out the two sentences in the display box on page 17. Challenge the students to be alert for vivid, active verbs.

Now have them turn to Exercise A, page 18.

A. Have students complete this exercise. Check and discuss. With less able students, you may wish to suggest additional letters, for example, in swallowed, letters 4 and 5 are both "l."

1. (a) swallowed
   (b) devoured
   (c) pecked
   (d) nibbled
   (e) gobbled

2. (a) pursued
   (b) trailed
   (c) chased
   (d) shadowed

3. (a) marched
   (b) ambled
   (c) plodded
   (d) strutted

B. Start the students working by doing Exercises 1 and 2 orally in class. They should then be able to do 3–10 easily.

1. beat—strum—tune—blow
2. placed—set—perched—positioned
3. scowled—pouted—snarled
4. raised—lifted—hoisted—brandished
5. wept—sobbed—whimpered—moaned
6. grabbed—snatched—seized—captured
7. recognized—noticed—spied—observed
8. rise—hover—loom
9. recaptured—retrieved—recovered—snatched
10. roared—yelled—bellowed—screamed

C. If possible, have a class set of dictionaries available for this exercise. Students can look up the meanings of the words on their own, but each word should be discussed. Point out that action verbs add power and force to our writing and speaking.

> **shuttlecock** (n.)—first used in 1522 to denote the rubber-nose "birdie" used in badminton. (Students should all be familiar with this definition.) In 1687, the *verb* form was used to describe the action of tossing something to and fro, just as players hit the "birdie" to and fro.

Students should be able to complete the exercise with little difficulty.

1. shuttlecock: to toss to and fro (also when used as a noun— the feathered "birdie" used in badminton)
2. yammer: to whine or complain persistently; to utter repeated cries of distress
3. bludgeon: to hit with a heavy object
4. zoom: to increase sharply
5. taunt: to jeer at; to challenge mockingly
6 and 7.   (Answers will vary.)
8. yammered
9. zoomed
10. shuttlecock

11. taunted
12. bludgeoned
13 and 14. (Answers will vary.)

VARIATIONS AND FOLLOW-UPS

1. **Extending Their Knowledge.** Bring a Roget's *Thesaurus* into class. Have one student look up the verb **walk** and read aloud the synonyms. Have another student list these on the chalkboard. Let the entire class discuss these. EXAMPLES: march, step, tread, pace, plod, promenade, trudge, strut, stride, tramp, toddle. Ask students to explain why these are SYNONYMS. (They all describe a method of walking.) Then ask them to explain why they are different. (Each describes a different method of walking.) If you have an extrovert in your class or a would-be actor, have that person act out a few of the synonyms listed and let the class guess which one is being acted out. This will emphasize the action quality of these verbs and differentiate them at the same time. If you like, continue with other verbs: talk, hit, paint, crush.

2. **Applying Their Knowledge.** Have students write one sentence using one of the words from one of the lists developed in Exercise 1. Then have them replace that word with other words on the same list. After each replacement, ask the students to explain how using that particular word changes the meaning of the sentence. This should help them to understand the importance of choosing the "best word" when they are writing.

STEP II, Chapter 5, Specific Verbs—Use Them!
Pages 22–25

A. Have students complete the exercise. Check and discuss. As you do, emphasize the extra power and force given by the action verbs they inserted.

1. devoured	4. sobbed	7. shadowed
2. pursued	5. yammered	8. ambled
3. strummed	6. observed	9. hovered
		10. perched

B. Have students complete the exercise. Check and discuss. Here you may wish to emphasize the variety of sentences created by different students.

1. The toddler punched the Doberman.
2. The raccoon gobbled the chocolate cake.
3. At midnight, the vagabond beat a drum and marched around the jail.
4. The thief snatched a bracelet from the counter and ran.
5. The zoo seemed melancholy as the lions moaned, the elephants whimpered, and the wolves wailed.

C. This exercise can be handled orally or in writing. Here are some suggested responses.

spoke	snarled	muttered	whined	whimpered
whispered	declared	cried	roared	bellowed
asserted	uttered	expressed	stated	protested

D. After students have completed this exercise, have several of them read their work aloud. Ask the class to point out variations in their answers and to discuss how these variations changed the tone of the paragraph from student to student. You may wish to read the following paragraph as an example.

Only half-conscious, I **spied** for the first time the Abominable Snowman. He **loomed** above me. He **scowled.** He **brandished** one huge arm like a club.

"Grr!" he **snarled.**

"Grr!" I **muttered.**

He **snatched** my baseball cap and **perched** it on his own gargantuan head. Now I really had a problem. Pride ordered me to **retrieve** my cap. Prudence suggested otherwise. Prudence won.

"It's all yours," I **whimpered** finally.

VARIATIONS AND FOLLOW-UPS

1. **Practice.** Have each student write a two or three-sentence paragraph describing an action event: a play in football, the baking of a cake, the start of a race, etc. After they have finished, have each exchange with another student. Now ask them to replace the action

verbs with new action verbs. Return the students' papers and let the original writers decide whether the replaced words increase or decrease the power of the writing. (This will vary.)

2. **Increasing Insight.** Ask each student *why* he or she chose a particular topic to write about in Exercise 1. What does this indicate about the writer? (*Writing about football or baseball or a race probably indicates the writer is an athlete or interested in athletics; writing about the baking of a cake indicates an interest in cooking, etc.*) Now carry this a step further. In writing about a football play (for example), who used the stronger, more colorful verbs: the person who plays or knows a lot about football or the one who doesn't? Obviously, the former. Again this shows how our interests and strengths influence our writing. It also indicates that we write best when we write about something we know well.

3. **Game.** Play the game described on page 15 of this manual, but this time alternate between specific nouns and action verbs. New categories for nouns: colors; meats; insects; games played with a ball; bakery goods, etc.

   Categories for action verbs: walk; talk; cry; fly; throw; stumble, etc. A couple of rounds of this game will review specific nouns, strengthen knowledge of action verbs, and emphasize the difference between the two.

STEP II, Chapter 6, Specific Verbs: Use Them In *Your* Writing!
Pages 26–30

A. 1. After students have completed this exercise, divide them into groups of four to exchange paragraphs and read them. Ask each group to choose one of the four as the best, the funniest, or the most unusual. Then have the "best" paragraphs read aloud to the entire class. Follow each reading with a discussion about how the verbs used contributed to the tone or mood of the paragraph.

2. Discuss briefly the difference between the two methods of organization the students have used: moving from a generalization to supporting details; and now moving from supporting details to a generalization. Point out that the first method is more logical and presents material clearly, but that the second allows for a slow building up of suspense and curiosity that will be satisfied only in the last sentence. Both methods are good; sometimes students will want to use one, sometimes the other.

B. The only problem with this exercise may lie in part 2. If students have never worked with body language, they may need a few minutes of relevant discussion. Start with facial expressions: a scowl, a smile, raised eyebrows, narrowed eyes. What does each indicate about the mood of the person? *A scowl*: anger or annoyance; *a smile*: pleasure; *raised eyebrows*: shock, surprise; *narrowed eyes*: suspicion, dislike. Go on to tone of voice: *high* and *shrill*: panic or excitement; *stammering*: hesitation or fear. Go on to body movements: *arms crossed over the chest*: hostility, disagreement; *a tapping foot*: impatience; *tapping fingers*: impatience or disagreement, etc. Students should now be able to complete the exercise.

C. Before students begin this exercise, discuss the format briefly. Point out that the date always appears in the upper-right-hand corner; that "Dear . . ." almost always introduces the salutation; that with handwritten letters, the first line of each paragraph is indented; that a complimentary closing is used—in this case, "As ever" is lined up with the date; and that the signature follows the complimentary closing. In this way, you have covered (probably as a review) the format for a friendly letter.

After they have completed the letter, ask a few volunteers to read theirs aloud for class discussion or collect and grade as a quiz.

Point out WRITING TECHNIQUE 2 on page 30.

VARIATIONS AND FOLLOW-UPS

1. **Point of View.** Ask students to replace the verbs in the following sentences to suit the indicated points of view.
   (a) Maria TOUCHED the crystal vase.

   (from the fearful storeowner's point of view): _____
   (pawed)

(from someone who knows Maria's love for glass):

_____ (caressed)
(b)   Six-year-old Jimmy HIT his four-year-old sister.

(from Jimmy's point of view): _____ (tapped)

(from his sister's point of view): _____ (punched)

2.   **Supporting Details to a Generalization.** If your students need more work on this method of organization, give them a list of supporting details. Here's one example:

Ellen washed and dried her hair.
She put on her prettiest dress and new shoes.
She watched the clock anxiously, fearing she would be late.

What generalization can be drawn? Several possibilities include: Ellen was going out with her favorite boyfriend, or with a new boyfriend, or to a school dance.

Ask a volunteer to give at least three details and let the class provide one or more generalizations that fit the details.

STEP III, Chapter 7, Apt Adjectives: Learn Them!
Pages 32–37

PREPARATION

Introduce your students to the Third Step to Better Writing—Apt Adjectives. Remind them that adjectives help the writer to describe something or someone more exactly. Have the students turn to page 32. Call their attention to the display box, and discuss why the first sentence is clever and much better than the second.

Most of your students will already know what an adjective is, but they can always profit from review. Remind them that an ADJECTIVE is a word that describes a person, place, or thing. Then have them list—or have one student list—on the chalkboard as many adjectives as they can that might be used to describe a house.

Be sure they include the various categories of adjectives suitable for describing a house. For example:

color: white; green; etc.
size: large; small; etc.
shape: square; rectangular; etc.
appearance: pretty; formidable; etc.

Point out that all these are adjectives because they *describe* a thing, that is, a "house." They also *modify* the word "house."

Before students begin working on this exercise, spend a few minutes discussing with them both **alliteration** and **puns**. The first is a useful technique that they can use occasionally in their writing; the second should amuse them and sharpen their awareness of words.

Alliteration: Ask the students for examples. Let them be as silly as they like, but encourage their use of different sounds: bouncing baby boy; dark and dreadful door; rare and radiant writing. The last gives you the opportunity to remind students that it is the *sound* that is important, not the *letter*.

Puns: Many people groan when they hear a pun. Let your students do so, too. It's part of the fun! Here are a few to share with them for mutual enjoyment.

No matter how long a rock has been in your backyard, don't take it for granite.

Q. What is a little dog suffering from chills?
A. A pupsickle.

A mermaid, as everyone knows, is a deep-she fish.

Going to the dentist can be a drilling experience.

After a dogsled ride in Canada, Prince Charles commented: "That just sleighed me."

A. Have the students proceed with Exercise A on page 33. Invite them to share their original responses as well as those which are now, or have been used, on TV.

Family Feud	*Real People*	*Romper Room*
Love Boat	*Candid Camera*	*Tic Tac Dough*
Twilight Zone	*Star Search*	*Different Strokes*
Wonder Woman		

Alliteration: *Family Feud; Romper Room*
Pun: *Tic Tac Dough*
Apt: (Answers will vary).

For this exercise, you may prefer to have your students answer question 1, pause to check the answer, and then discuss it. They should then be more efficient in handling the second question. This exercise should sharpen thinking as well as grammar.

B. 1. **Dream** is an apt adjective because it forms alliteration with **Delta** and at the same time exploits the fact that we all have dreams and hope to have our dreams come true.

2. "Smog-filled Prague" would be more accurate; but **smoggy** conveys the heavy, messy feeling of smog and therefore is apt.

3. **Old** and **new** set up a sharp contrast and set the stage for the pun in "platform." Therefore **old** in this context is apt, rather than dated.

4. Because **beer** and **budget** are alliterative; **champagne** and **budget** are not. The ad is aimed at people who have to watch their money—hence the emphasis on beer rather than on champagne. The ad is catchy because it uses alliteration.

5. No. The power of the headline lies in the contrast between the huge and powerful Air Command and the tiny bird that stopped it. Using a huge, winged bird would decrease the contrast and therefore the effectiveness.

C. Spend plenty of time discussing the material in the box that precedes C on page 35 and in the introductory material to C. You may wish to stop after each part for immediate checking and discussion.

1. **Orange**

orange; gold; copper
round; rotund; spherical; globular
sweet; tangy; juicy; sharp
soft; rough; firm; smooth
sweet-smelling; pungent; scented; bitter

a spherical, copper orange, juicy, soft, and pungent

25

2. **Pencil**

> yellow; green; white
> narrow; long; hexagonal; straight
> woodlike; dull; biting
> smooth; glossy; bumpy (if pencil has been chewed)
> like lead; bland; like wood shavings
>
> a hexagonal yellow pencil that smells and tastes like
> wood and is bumpy from my frequent gnawing on it

3. (a) brilliant; glossy; glittering; radiant; shimmering
    (b) deafening; earsplitting; piercing; clangorous; powerful
    (c) grimy; squalid; disreputable; dust-covered; filthy

D. If possible, have a class set of dictionaries available for this exercise. After the students have located and written the definitions, discuss them with the students. All five words are worth adding to their speaking, listening, and writing vocabularies.

1. warlike; hostile
2. of tremendous size
3. threatening; foreshadowing evil
4. filled with great joy or a sense of triumph
5. honest; unprejudiced; unposed
6 and 7.   (Answers will vary.)
8. exultant
9. candid
10. ominous
11. gargantuan
12. belligerent
13 and 14.   (Answers will vary.)

VARIATIONS AND FOLLOW-UPS

1. **Alliteration.** Almost all students enjoy working with alliteration. Have them write sentences in which every word (or almost every word) begins with the same sound. If they do well, have them try alliterative couplets . . . nonsense verses, something like this:

Silly Sally sure is sweet,
Strolling down the starlit street.

2. **Puns.** (For more able students only; others may find it frustrating.)
    Point out that many puns rest on the near similarity in sound of
    two unrelated words. One example:

    pool and *fool* (There's no pool like an old pool.)

    Some puns rest on a word that has two distinct meanings. Such
    as:
    pen (writing instrument and jail). The two prisoners became pen
    pals.
    comb (instrument to make hair neat or the crest of a rooster)
    A rooster is the neatest bird; he always has a comb!

    To show your students what can be done with puns, write on the
    chalkboard this quatrain by the poet Thomas Hood.

    > His death, which happened in his berth,
    >   At forty-odd befell;
    > They went and told the sexton
    >   And the sexton tolled the bell.

    Suggest that students create sentences using puns. If they show some
    skill at this, let them progress to couplets or quatrains based on puns.

3. **Media.** If possible, bring in a set of newspapers, all the same issue.
    (If this isn't possible, ask students to bring in a copy of the local
    newspaper, same issue.) Then ask them to check the headlines and
    find forceful or colorful adjectives.

4. **Media.** Use the same set of newspapers used in Exercise 3. This
    time select one short story and ask the students to circle every ad-
    jective in the story. (This would be a good time to impress on them
    that "a," "an," and "the" are adjectives, although they indicate
    or point out rather than describe.)

STEP III, Chapter 8, Apt Adjectives: Use Them!
Pages 38–41

Have the students do Exercises A and B on page 38. (The answers will vary.)

C. Have the students consider the use of appropriate adjectives for each situation described.

    1. weary   4. guilt-stricken
    2. terrified   5. nervous
    3. skeptical

D. After the students have completed Exercise D, discuss *why* one particular answer is better than another. For example, "broiling" we associate with a hamburger sizzling and sputtering and therefore it seems considerably hotter than "hot."

    1. broiling   4. battered
    2. ominous   5. huge
    3. exultant

E. Reading and talking about the introduction to this exercise should help your students use their imaginations to dream up interesting adjective-noun combinations. They should then be ready to work on their own. Later, a discussion of the results should help them to determine which combinations are really serendipitous (unexpectedly happy)!

    Some possibilities: thundering appetite; spicy letter; crisp advice; rickety welcome

F. Have students complete this exercise. Then have several revised paragraphs read aloud, followed by a discussion of the effectiveness of the adjectives inserted. Point out again that different people will choose different words because each person has a unique set of experiences to draw from.

    fantastic time; **congenial** fellow; **breathtaking** experience; was **unforgettable; intricate** sand; **colorful** tribal; **vivid** colors; **magnificent** time

VARIATIONS AND FOLLOW-UPS

1. **Media.** Using the same set of newspapers as those in Chapter 7 (or a new set), select one short item and ask students to circle all adjectives. Then ask them to try to improve the story by adding (or replacing) a few of the adjectives.

2. **Media.** If a set of *Time* magazines is available, give one to each student. If not, choose one particular story, preferably a short one written in *Time's* inimitable style. Ask the students to identify the best, most unusual adjectives and to explain why each is (or is not) effective. With more able students only: suggest that each try to write a short item following *Time's* style.

3. **Dictionary Work.** Distribute dictionaries. Write on the chalkboard one noun, perhaps "carnival." Have students browse through the dictionary for five minutes to find unusual and exciting adjectives that might be used to describe the word. Write the results on the chalkboard and discuss.

STEP III, Chapter 9, Apt Adjectives: Use Them in *Your* Writing!
Pages 42–45

A. Have students complete the exercise. Later, have volunteers read paragraphs, allowing members of the class to guess the objects or events being described. (Answers will vary.)

B. Have students complete this exercise. Check and discuss. (If you are interested in this topic, collect copies of the students' work and file until later in the year. They could then be revised and edited into a booklet.)

C. You may wish to discuss with the students the kind of thank-you notes they might like to receive. Encourage them to use apt adjectives to describe the gift. Have the students refer to page 30 of the text for a model for a friendly note. A sample letter appears here for your convenience.

Dear Aunt Mary,

Thank you for the dynamic crimson scarf that you sent for my birthday. I love it, and it makes me glow even in November gales! This winter's dark days will be brightened by its warmth and color.

I wear the scarf frequently, Aunt Mary, and when I do, I think of you and your love. Thanks so much.

Your loving niece,
Eloise

VARIATIONS AND FOLLOW-UPS

1. **Game.** Have the students take out a piece of scrap paper. Then ask them to give an adjective for each of the following categories:

    (a) a color (e.g., red)
    (b) a size (e.g., large)
    (c) a shape (e.g., triangular)
    (d) an adjective describing a character trait (e.g., honest)
    (e) another adjective describing a character trait (e.g., happy)

    Now read the following sentences aloud and ask the students to insert the adjective they wrote. Students can enjoy this silently, but if there is good rapport among class members, they will enjoy it even more if they share the results.

    (a) _____ is the color of my true love's hair.

    (b) My ego is exceedingly _____ .

    (c) I would like to be _____ .

    (d) I am _____ , but

    (e) I am not _____ .

    If the students enjoyed this game, let them divide into groups and prepare additional rounds.

2. **Game.** Play this "Twenty Questions" game. Have one student think of an object and give you a slip of paper with the name of the object written on it. Next let another student ask a question that includes an *adjective*:

>   Is it round?
>   Is it soft?
>   Is it red?

After the first question is answered with a "yes" or a "no," have a second student ask a question, a third, etc., up to twenty. The aim of the students, of course, is to identify the object in as few questions as possible.

3. **Advertisement.** Bring in your local newspaper and point out a few ads with apt adjectives. Challenge the students to write an ad for something they would like: a motorcycle, a computer, a pair of designer jeans. In their ads they should use apt adjectives that will capture a reader's attention and encourage the reader to purchase the item.

Point out to the students WRITING TECHNIQUE 3 on page 45. Review this technique before going on to the next writing assignment.

WRITING TIME—I
Pages 46–48

You may wish to read this section aloud before students begin work. Point out that the three celebrations described actually take place every year. Help students to enjoy the idea of "organized nonsense." Possibly winters are hard in Sault Ste. Marie, and people greet the coming of spring enthusiastically. Possibly Columbia, Tennessee, finds the mule a valuable animal and helper. The pancake race is harder. Perhaps some early settlers in Liberal, Kansas, came from Olney, England, and brought the tradition with them. You might even ask the students to dream up a special celebration that would suit their community. Students should enjoy both learning about these unusual celebrations and writing about them.

31

Sample essay, incorporating *A*, *B*, *C*, and *D*:

LET'S CELEBRATE

Given any reason at all, people will do the weirdest things. What's more, they'll do them every year and brag about them!

In Sault Ste. Marie, Michigan, the whole town gathers every March 20th to wave away winter and to hail the spring. Hundreds of people cheer wildly as a seven-foot paper snowman is burned to the tune of "I Don't Want to Set the World on Fire," and a few aspiring writers read aloud poems dripping with sunshine, robin song, and skies ever blue.

Columbia, Tennessee, takes note of the coming warm weather with a still wilder ritual. In April every year, one day is devoted to that stubborn, contrary, and rather ridiculous four-legged creature, the mule. During the daylight hours a mule parade sends every kid into ecstasy; and mule competitions and mule races rage wildly. But the highlight of the day is the "most outrageous lie" contest in which both adults and children vie fiercely for the honor of being proclaimed the biggest liar.

The midwesterners of Liberal, Kansas, don't wait until spring for their annual hijinks. Each year on Shrove Tuesday (preceding Ash Wednesday), a contingent of the married women meet, all armed with skillets holding pancakes. They then run a 415-yard race, occasionally flipping a pancake along the way. (Losing a pancake means losing the race!) Nowadays the women of Liberal race against the women of Olney, England, and both towns give high honors to the international winner.

Yes, whether it's burning a paper snowman, or telling whoppers, or running pancake races, people *do* do the darnedest things—even in public! Why? Who knows? Maybe to attract tourists—maybe to make money—but, most likely, just to have a bit of fun!

FOLLOW-UP

1. **Research.** To develop research skills with your students, have them track down other annual weird celebrations held in the United States (or even around the world). Some possible sources:

   almanacs of various kinds
   newspapers (especially *USA Today*)
   magazines (introduce them to *Reader's Guide to Periodical Literature*)
   Books of Days

Your school librarian can probably suggest other sources. The topic is fun, and your students should enjoy playing detective and tracking down this material.

2. **Writing.** If their research is successful, have the students write about each celebration and choose the best versions. These can be collected into a booklet and given to the library. Knowing that others are reading and enjoying their writing should motivate students to improve their writing and to write more.

PREPARATION FOR UNIT TEST ONE (See test booklet.) For your convenience the answers appear on p. 129 of this manual.

TEST PREPARATION

1. Review technical vocabulary: especially—noun, verb, adjective, generalization, details, synonyms, alliteration, puns, general, specific.

2. Review general vocabulary. See pages 6, 21, and 37 in text.

3. Review thoroughly the three parts of speech studied: noun, verb, and adjective. Review with the students by asking for:
    (a) adjectives that might describe a particular noun
         EXAMPLE: "dog"—old, battered, playful, etc.
    (b) nouns that might follow a particular adjective
         EXAMPLE: "sparkling"—eyes, dialogue, sunbeam, etc.
    (c) verbs that might follow a particular subject
         EXAMPLE: "The dinosaur"—roared, trampled, snorted, etc.

4. Review moving from the general to the specific. Ask the students for a specific noun for:
    (a) body of water (Pacific Ocean, Lake Erie)
    (b) city (Pittsburgh)
    (c) candy (Three Musketeers)
    (d) bread (pumpernickel)

Continue reviewing until most students seem completely at ease with the use of specific nouns.

NOTE: All Unit Tests are divided into two parts: Part I, testing memory; and Part II, testing application in writing. Each test may be given alone or may be combined by adjusting the number of points assigned to each question.

UNIT TWO

STEP IV, Chapter 10, Agile Adverbs: Learn Them!
Pages 50–54

PREPARATION

Adverbs tend to be mysterious critters to young people. Suggest that they think of an adjective and an adverb as a brother and a sister: the adjective describes nouns and pronouns, the adverb describes verbs, adjectives, and other adverbs. Have them list and write on the chalkboard some of the verbs they worked with in Chapter 2. Precede each verb with a pronoun.

> He walks.
> She talks.
> He eats.
> She runs.

Next have the students suggest adverbs (usually words ending in –*ly*) that would match each verb. Write these after the verbs. Challenge them to find four adverbs for each verb without repeating one.

> He walks—quickly—slowly—painfully—wearily
> She talks—rapidly—gleefully—tearfully—grimly
> He eats—greedily—enthusiastically—unwillingly—sparingly
> She runs—madly—swiftly—triumphantly—awkwardly

Introduce the Fourth Step to Better Writing—Agile Adverbs. Point out that adverbs tell *how*, *when*, or *where* an action is done, and usually end in –*ly*. Call the students' attention to the display box on page 50. Explain the reference to "Tom Swifties."

A. 1. Have students complete the exercise. Check and discuss.

(a)	skillfully	(c)	brilliantly
(b)	fiercely	(d)	carelessly

2. Read the introductory material aloud. Have students complete the exercise. Check and discuss.
   (a) soon
   (b) later
   (c) fast
   (d) here
   (e) tight
3. Read the material in the box aloud. Have the students complete the exercise. Check and discuss. At first students may need help finding the word an adverb modifies, but after working on a few exercises, they should become more proficient.
   (a) extremely—modifies angry
   (b) nostalgically—modifies talked
   (c) gently—modifies said
   (d) more rapidly—modifies painted
   (e) very—modifies shy

B.   This section should be sheer fun. Do much (or all) of it orally, letting your students enjoy the "Tom Swifties." Things may get a bit noisy, but adverbs will never again be awesome mysteries to your students! Items 11, 12, and 13 should be worked on individually, of course, but if the students develop a few good "Tom Swifties," they will love trying them on others—and even on you!

   1. absently
   2. cuttingly
   3. brokenly
   4. sourly
   5. airily
   6. candidly
   7. darkly
   8. winningly
   9. sharply
   10. tartly
   11, 12, and 13. (Answers will vary.)

VARIATIONS AND FOLLOW-UPS

1. **Game.** Try a variation of the "Wheel of Fortune" TV game. Write a "Tom Swiftie" sentence on the chalkboard, putting in place of an adverb a square or box for each letter. Have one student suggest a letter. If the letter is in the adverb, place it in the correct box, and

the student gets a chance to choose another letter. If the letter is not in the adverb, the student loses his or her turn, and another student tries. The student who guesses the adverb correctly is, of course, the winner. The game will review adverbs, improve spelling skills, and sharpen thinking skills.

2. **Game.** Distribute to students four small pieces of paper. On one, ask them to write a noun; on the second, an active verb; on the third, a vivid adjective; on the fourth, a forceful adverb. Collect all nouns and place them in one container; all verbs in another container, etc. Then have each student select one piece of paper from each container and use the four words selected to create a sentence. The results should be hilarious, and students will be reviewing the four basic parts of speech at the same time.

STEP IV, Chapter 11, Agile Adverbs: Use Them!
Pages 55–58

A.   Have students complete the exercise. Check and discuss.

1. wearily	6. greedily
2. eerily	7. painfully
3. enthusiastically	8. skillfully
4. electronically	9. desperately
5. fiendishly	10. cleverly

B.   This exercise forces students to use judgment in selecting the adverb that fits both the sentence and the celebrity. Discussing why one adverb is better than the other should help them to develop an ear for language. Handle orally or in writing.

1. finally
2. always
3. vividly
4. upside down
5. magnificently

C. Have students complete the exercise. Check and discuss.

confidently predicted   swore **silently**
falling **lightly**   lay **helplessly**
inched **timidly**   dangling **dangerously**

D. Have students complete the exercise. Check and discuss.

1. exceedingly   4. remarkably
2. astonishingly   5. decidedly
3. incredibly

E. (The material used in this paragraph is true, taken from a newspaper account.) Have students complete the exercise. Before you go over the answers, remind them to check each adverb to see if an "a" or "an" should precede it. Have a few paragraphs read aloud and discuss the effectiveness of some of the choices.

decidedly ordinary   **furiously** angry
cruelly sharp   **markedly** cautious
exceedingly annoyed

VARIATIONS AND FOLLOW-UPS

1. **Using Repetition.** Ask students to review the use of repetition in Exercise C, page 56. Then have them write a short paragraph on any topic, in which a key word or phrase is used at least *three* times. When they have finished, have them take a few minutes to revise, following this check list.

Did you use one word or phrase at least three times? (If you did not, do so.)
Check your nouns. Are they specific? (If not, replace.)
Check your verbs. Are they active? Are they forceful? (If not, replace.)
Check your adjectives. Are they exact? Are they apt? Are they colorful? (If not, replace.)
Check your adverbs. Are they forceful? Are they exact? (If not, replace.)

Now have the students revise their paragraphs and copy them neatly on a clean sheet of paper. Collect the papers. Read the paragraphs rapidly and choose a few of the most clever to read aloud. Or you may wish to grade the papers as a writing exercise.

2. **Sentence Arranging.** Give the students the following words. They may be written on the chalkboard.

NOUNS: boy, bull
VERB: struck
ADJECTIVES: the, mad, small
ADVERB: furiously

Ask the students to arrange the words into a sentence—then to rearrange them into a second sentence—and a third—and a fourth—and a fifth. Some possible sentences:

The small boy struck the mad bull furiously.
The mad boy struck the small bull furiously.
The small bull struck furiously the mad boy.
The mad bull furiously struck the small boy.
Furiously, the small, mad bull struck the boy.
The small, mad boy furiously struck the bull.

This "game" can be played over and over, using different nouns, verbs, adjectives, and adverbs. It will help students to learn the four basic parts of speech and will give them an understanding of the structure of a sentence.

STEP IV, Chapter 12, Agile Adverbs: Use Them in *Your* Writing!
Pages 59–63

A. With less able students especially, spend a few minutes discussing what *related events* means . . . perhaps three times when they played with a friend, or three times they were hurt playing baseball, or three school days they especially enjoyed. The important thing is to get them to think in terms of related events. Once they have grasped this concept, they should have little difficulty with this exercise.

One possible follow-up: Break into small groups. Let the students read paragraphs to group members and select one for reading to the class. After each reading of a "best" paragraph, discuss the use of good adjectives and adverbs.

B. Before students work on this exercise, you may find it helpful to spend a little time discussing the term chronological. List three things you did today—chronologically: get out of bed, dress, go to school; list three things you did in the past week—chronologically.

1. (Answers will vary.)
2. (1)   (3)
   (5)   (2)
   (6)   (4)
                (7)
3. (2 and 3)
   (6)
   (7)

4. The Fourth of July. The date rings resoundingly to Americans since that first July 4th in 1776. Then, when the Continental Congress adopted the Declaration of Independence in Philadelphia, we took our freedom into our own hands and set up a mighty roar. We roared again on July 4th, 1777, the first anniversary, with a barrage of fireworks that splashed glowing paint across the skies above Philadelphia. We roared for about two centuries with small firecrackers by day and community fireworks at night. Then, in the 1950s, many states banned the use of firecrackers by individuals, and community fireworks became even more important. Today, here in Merryville, we hold true to tradition, celebrating the Fourth with a parade, a ball game, and a brilliant display of fireworks. As we "ooh" and "aah" at the bursts of sparkling colors, our hearts pound fiercely, for we are still roaring our delight, still holding our freedom securely in our own hands.

C. Here, too, the students will profit from a little preexercise discussion. What is a "whopper"? Who tells them? About what? You may wish to tell them a few Paul Bunyan "whoppers."

Paul Bunyan was a lumberjack who was incredibly huge and powerful. He owned a tremendously large blue ox called Babe. In fact, everything about Paul Bunyan was BIG! Once he was in the Adirondacks and came across Huggard's Pond. It was really late, and Paul's men were starved, so Paul had an idea. He dumped a few loads of beans into the pond and a whole lot of cold pork, too. Then he built fires on the banks of the pond, and he ended up with a pond of bean soup. Real tasty, it was, too. They say Paul and his men ate every bit of that soup, and when they were finished, the pond was plumb dry. (For other "whoppers" consult Thompson's *Body, Boots, and Britches* or any other collection of folklore.)

When your students are still hungry for more, challenge them to write an extravagant whopper of their own.

Later they will enjoy exchanging papers and reading one another's wild tales.

Point out WRITING TECHNIQUE 4 on page 63. This may be a good time to review the previous WRITING TECHNIQUES which have been taught.

VARIATIONS AND FOLLOW-UPS

1. **Folklore.** For students interested in Paul Bunyan, suggest a little research into the folklore of your own area. (The librarian should be able to help them.) Let them find some good examples and then write them as short, short stories. These stories, after being revised, can be made into a booklet or submitted to the school or local newspapers.

2. **Research.** Have students talk to parents and older residents of the community to learn about major events: fires, renovations, participation in wars, etc. Remind them to date each event. Later the students can pool their findings and arrange them chronologically. A few students may be interested in consulting books of local history to add a few facts about the founding of the town. Then the class can write the history of the community, using the nouns, verbs, adjectives, and adverbs learned to date.

3. **Game.** Try the "Wheel of Fortune" game again. This time give only one clue: whether the word is a noun, verb, adjective, or adverb. Set up the necessary number of blocks or boxes on the chalkboard.

$$\boxed{||||}\text{ (for a five-letter word)}$$

Follow the procedure outlined on page 33 of this guide. This game will review the four basic parts of speech and spelling and will improve thinking skills.

STEP V, Chapter 13, Personal Pronouns: Learn Them!

Pages 65–68

Introduce the students to the Fifth Step to Better Writing—Personal Pronouns. Discuss the two sentences in the display box on page 65. Explain how "I" and "he" or "she" make a difference in our point of view.

Review the definition of a pronoun: a word that takes the place of a noun. Read the introductory material (pages 66–67) with your students, stopping frequently to ask questions and to answer others.

Give students some oral drill by reading the following sentences aloud and asking them to replace italicized nouns with pronouns.

1. *Melissa* hit *Jim* with *Melissa's* purse.
2. *Jack* called *Jenny* and asked *Jenny* to return *Jack's* letter.
3. *Jean* and *Ellen* took *Bill* to the store.
4. *Steve* carried the *toddlers* to the *toddlers'* car.
5. When *Rosie* scared the bear, the *bear* dropped the *bear's* lunch.

A. Have students complete the exercise. Check and discuss.

1. He—her
2. We
3. you—your
4. theirs
5. I—I—I—her

42

B. Read and discuss with students notes 1, 2, and 3. They should then have little trouble completing Exercise 4. Check answers and discuss.

4. Morty and **I**   to Morty and **me**
   he was penalized   all of **us**
   he dropped   **my** name's Millie
   its way   **we** heard
   their sponsor   **they're** sputtering
   us adventurers   **you're** driving
   two of **us**   Morty and **me**
   she looked   **we** M&Ms

VARIATIONS AND FOLLOW-UPS

1. **Spelling Bee.** Hold a fast round or two of a spelling bee limited to pronouns. Read a sentence that includes a pronoun; ask student 1 to identify and spell the pronoun. If the choice and spelling are correct, move on to student 2. Any student who misses is "out." Emphasize tricky pronouns: "their" and "they're"—"your" and "you're"—"its" and "it's" but include all pronouns occasionally. (If you can eliminate pronoun spelling errors, especially those of the three pairs listed above, you will have helped your students immensely.)

2. **Practice.** Duplicate copies of a short newspaper story. Ask the students to write two versions: one in which all nouns are changed to pronouns, and one in which all pronouns are changed to nouns. Ask them what is incorrect with both versions. (All nouns: sentences are unwieldy, awkward, and repetitive; all pronouns: meaning is often ambiguous, not clear, and vital information is not given.) Emphasize the need to use pronouns correctly and clearly.

STEP V, Chapter 14, Personal Pronouns: Use Them!
Pages 69–74

Point of view is one of the most important aspects of writing, yet it is often unfamiliar to students. Read aloud the introductory material (pp.

(69–70). Then spend ten minutes helping the students understand what **point of view** is. These exercises may help.

1. Imagine an ordinary kitchen; see yourself in it. How big is the table in relation to your size? the chairs? the sink? the stove?
2. Imagine the same kitchen, but this time imagine it as a twelve-foot giant might see it. How would he go about washing his hands? Could he sit down? What problems would he have frying an egg?
3. Imagine the same kitchen, but this time imagine a two-year-old in it. How does everything look? What problems would she have getting a drink of water? How would she get an apple that is in the center of the table?

   Help your students to see that although the kitchen remains the same, it looks different to three different people. Each has a distinctive **point of view.**
4. An eight-year-old boy is riding a bike. He's trying to get away from his four-year-old sister who is chasing him. He rides in circles, getting madder and madder. Suddenly he crashes into the garage door, breaking his bike. How does he see this incident? Whom does he consider responsible for the broken bike?
5. How does the four-year-old see this incident? Does she feel responsible for the broken bike?
6. How does his mother or father assign responsibility?

Again—the same incident, but three different points of view. Students should be ready now for the exercises.

A. Have the students complete the exercise. Check and discuss.

1(a)   3rd person is better, since someone else can describe our faces better than we can. *They* see us; *we* rarely see ourselves truly.

2(a)   3rd person is better, since the 1st-person statement sounds boastful.

3(a or b)   Both are possible, but 1st person is a little more effective, because it is poignant—an old person realizing the encroachment of old age.

44

4(a)	3rd person is essential, since the patient could hardly know her or his eyes were blank and his or her mouth was open.
5(b)	1st person is probably better, since the informal chatty sentences indicate a 1st-person approach.
6(a)	From a 3rd-person point of view—because someone else sees physical characteristics more clearly than we do.
(b)	From a 1st-person point of view—since only we can get inside ourselves and explain how we feel.

B. Have students complete this exercise. Check and discuss.

1. 3rd person—because a young man in a coma could hardly describe his own condition or the surrounding circumstances.
2. 1st person—because a sci-fi writer can do things an ordinary writer can't do, such as getting inside an unconscious person's mind and expressing what is going on there.
3. Probably 3rd person—a 1st-person description of bulging muscles would sound boastful.
4. 1st person—the "I was there" approach would add power and immediacy to the writing.
5. 1st person—essential for a recounting of memories.

C. Have students complete the exercise. Check and discuss.

"Go ahead," Janey told herself. "Take it . . . before you turn chicken and run."

She moved her hand stealthily toward the gold watch.

Outside Kahn's Department Store, sleet had turned the city's skyscrapers to glittering ice palaces. She could pawn a watch like this, get enough for a room for a few days, maybe even for a week. She touched it. Warmth shot through her. She thought of a bed, four walls, quiet. Then she withdrew her hand abruptly. A few yards away, a man in a trench coat stood, his eyes dark and cold.

"Pretty," she mumbled inadequately and walked away out into the storm.

D. Have the students complete this exercise. (With less able students, pause to check and discuss after *each* answer.) (Answers will vary considerably.)

VARIATIONS AND FOLLOW-UPS

1. **Practice.** If students need more work in grasping **point of view,** give a few examples for them to consider.

   EXAMPLE: Bob and Dave are working together in school at a personal computer. Bob is actually operating it at the moment, but both boys are playing, nudging and shoving each other. The monitor falls and breaks, and repairs will cost about $300. Describe the incident (and responsibility) from:

   (a) Bob's point of view
   (b) Dave's point of view
   (c) the teacher's point of view
   (d) Bob's father's point of view

   EXAMPLE: It's snowing heavily. Already there are 24 inches of snow on the ground, the winds are strong, and the temperature is about 25 degrees. Describe the weather (and its probable results) from the point of view of:

   (a) a ten-year-old girl
   (b) an athletic twenty-year-old college student
   (c) a middle-aged woman who has to drive 23 miles to work
   (d) an old man who lives alone in an isolated house

   More examples can be given. Some students may enjoy setting up additional examples for other students to think about.

2. **Writing.** Tell your students about *Rashomon*. *Rashomon* was first a short story by R. Akutagawa, a Japanese writer. Later it was made into a prize-winning film and still later into a Broadway play.

   The story takes place in Kyoto, Japan, about a thousand years ago. A robber attacks a young couple. The husband is killed, the wife disappears, and the robber is arrested. What really happened? The story is told several times from different points of view—by the robber, the dead man (through his spirit), the young wife, a woodcarver (a witness), a wigmaker (who understands how the woodcarver's mind works), a priest, and a police deputy. Each lies; each sees the incident as upholding his or her own self-image.

Challenge your students to try a similar approach. Some possibilities:

(a) a teenage shoplifter (points of view: the teenager, a parent, the store owner, the police, a school friend, a younger brother or sister)

(b) a drunk driver hits a pedestrian who is paralyzed for life (points of view: the driver, the pedestrian, a member of the pedestrian's family, a member of the driver's family, a witness, a judge)

STEP V, Chapter 15, Personal Pronouns: Use Them in *Your* Writing!
Pages 75–80

Your students already know how to organize a paragraph chronologically (according to time). Now explain how they can organize it spatially (according to space).

In traveling across the United States, you might leave from the northeast, travel across the Midwest and far west to the West Coast, then return through the southwest, the southern central, and the southeast—making a circle tour. If you have a map of the United States available, point out a possible logical route—spatially logical.

Ask: If you want to describe this community spatially, how would you do it? (clockwise, counterclockwise, north to south, east to west—but *not* haphazardly)

If you want to describe a face spatially, how would you do it? (top to bottom, bottom to top)

By now, they should have grasped the concept of spatial organization and should be able to proceed to Exercise A.

A. Have students complete the exercise. Later, ask one or two students to read their paragraphs aloud. Discuss.

Sample answer:

Fourteen-year-old Allie paused at the entrance of the new Youth Center. She gasped with delight when she saw the gleaming new ping-pong table to the right, and her eyes opened even wider when she noticed just beyond it a dozen bright red and green card tables,

47

more than half already in use. Flashing lights and beeping noises caught her attention; straight ahead were several arcade games, each reacting violently as some youths pulled levers and pushed buttons. It was too much, too wonderful to take in. Her glance wandered to the left, to a basketball court with a shiny floor and snowy white nets, where a group of boys jumped and ran and threw a ball with great glee. It was almost a relief, Allie decided, to rest her eyes on a small lounge directly to her left. She walked into it, sank into a comfortable chair, and studied with joyful anticipation the books and magazines that rested on gleaming maple shelves. A Youth Center—and what a Youth Center! Maybe now. . . .

B. Have students complete the exercise. They will enjoy exchanging papers and reading one another's paragraphs.

C. Have students complete the exercise. Either have a few read and discussed or collect and grade, placing emphasis on the spatial organization.

VARIATIONS AND FOLLOW-UPS

1. **Media.** Ask each student to browse through one issue of a magazine and find a story or an article that is organized chronologically and one that is organized spatially. In each case, have the student skim the article and explain why chronological or spatial organization was used. This would be a good time to review the difference between fiction (specifically short stories) and nonfiction (articles). Usually the students will find that stories are organized chronologically, while articles are organized either chronologically or spatially.

2. **Spatial Planning.** Make available to all students a detailed map of Europe. Ask them to prepare a circle tour—one that begins and ends in the same city. They should include five countries and eight cities in the tour. Check their tours briefly to be sure they have developed tours that are *spatially* logical. Finally, have them write a brief paragraph about each tour that describes each location. (Later, if you like, bring in some travel brochures—available at any travel agency— and let them compare professional treatment to their own.)

Point out WRITING TECHNIQUE 5 on page 80.

STEP VI, Chapter 16, Purposeful Prepositions: Learn Them!

Pages 82–87

Introduce the Sixth Step to Better Writing—Purposeful Prepositions. Call attention to the two sentences in the display box on page 82. Invite the students to enjoy the humor of Earl Wilson's statement as well as his correct use of prepositions.

PREPARATION

Write on the chalkboard a list of commonly used prepositions.

in	near	under	with	until	for
on	beside	beneath	by	unless	despite
to	between	above	from	around	but
at	among	over	of	into	

Tell the class these are all prepositions. Ask them to figure out what else they have in common.

(a) Develop a phrase with *one* of the prepositions listed above:

the preposition plus a noun; e.g., on the table. Develop four more prepositional phrases.

(b) Form a sentence by placing "The boy walked" in front of each of the prepositional phrases.

(c) Study the five sentences. What does a preposition DO? (Shows relationship between one person or thing and another person or thing.)

You may wish to point out that a prepositional phrase is made up of a preposition plus a noun or a pronoun and possibly one or more adjectives. If a verb exists, it is not a prepositional phrase but a clause.

EXAMPLE: He waited (until dinner). (prepositional phrase)

He waited (until the game was over). (dependent clause)

49

A. Have students complete this exercise. Check and discuss.

1. It's — **in** the garbage can.
     under the refrigerator.
     near the dragon.
     above the moon.
     behind the birdbath.

2. The duck waddled — **into** the mud puddle.
     across the cornfield.
     beside the porcupine.
     over Pike's Peak.
     with difficulty.

3. The escaped convict hid — **in** a pickle barrel.
     between two daffodils.
     among the strawberries.
     at the prison gate.
     on the roof.

B. Explain that diagraming a sentence will help them to understand the structure of a sentence. Spend time reviewing diagraming with the students.

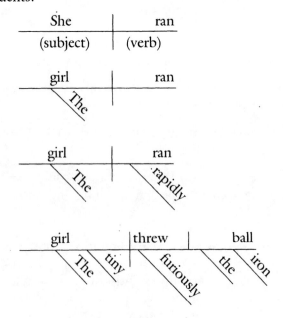

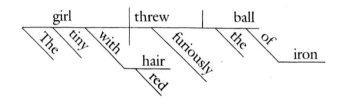

It is important not to make diagraming an end in itself. It is a means only—a way to help students *see* the structure of a sentence. Have the students complete this exercise. Check and discuss.

1. *with red hair*—adjective

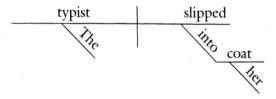

2. *into her coat*—adverb

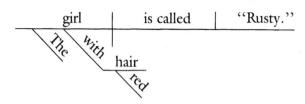

3. *in one teaspoon*—adverb

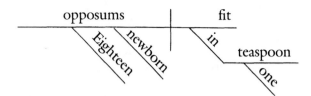

4. *in 1807*—adverb

5. *of ancient Rome*—adjective

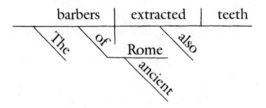

C. Have students complete the exercise. Check and discuss.

1. the world
2. the canister—noodles
3. the beach—shells
4. On the moon—toward the space ship
5. On the ice
6. in the red trunks—with one punch
7. at the dinosaur
8. off the road—into the ditch
9. to the peak—with a four-foot antenna
10. with the big ears—on the lollipops—at the refreshment stand

VARIATIONS AND FOLLOW-UPS

1. **Applying a Skill.** Have students take a paragraph from a newspaper or a magazine. Ask them to underline each preposition and to circle each prepositional phrase.

2. **Tour de Force.** For fun, challenge students to write a sentence that contains six prepositional phrases—if possible, more. (Of course, the sentence must make sense!)

    EXAMPLE: (In the morning) (with a bag) (of coins) (under his arm), the boy walked (up Fifth Avenue) (to the plaza) and (into a store) hoping to purchase a loaf (of bread). (eight prepositional phrases)

52

STEP VI, Chapter 17, Purposeful Prepositions: Use Them!

Pages 88–92

A. Combining sentences is a useful technique and should help students avoid using only short, choppy sentences. Begin by reading together the introductory material (page 88). Next handle the first sentence orally, asking for a volunteer to turn the second sentence into a prepositional phrase. Ask a second student to combine the two sentences, using the prepositional phrase suggested. Ask a third student to do the same thing, placing the prepositional phrase in a different part of the sentence. Caution students not to change the meaning of the sentence.

EXAMPLE: The doctor (in a low, gruff voice) told the patient the bad news.
(In a low, gruff voice), the doctor told the patient the bad news.
The doctor told the patient the bad news (in a low, gruff voice).

Repeat the procedure with sentence 2. If students seem to comprehend both the use of prepositions and the combining of sentences, they should then be able to complete the exercise successfully. Check and discuss.

1. In a low, gruff voice, the doctor told the patient the bad news.
2. With her surfboard under her arm, Michelle headed for the ocean and a joyful hour of riding the waves.
3. His little sister, Kerry, went with Jim to the hockey game.
4. At midnight three gnomes in small green suits perched on the highest hill.
5. Jessica went shopping for an umbrella and for a raincoat.
6. On Saturday ten boys went camping in the Adirondack woods.
7. With only his dog for company, a lost little boy found himself in a dark forest.
8. Jake traveled fifty miles in one day on a skateboard.
9. Mrs. Kee called the dentist for an appointment.
10. Carlos raked leaves for $4 an hour.

B. Read the example and revision. Challenge your students to rewrite the sentence by providing new prepositional phrases.

EXAMPLE: Two boys swam (in the backyard pool) (for twelve hours) (for fun).

Ask the students to rewrite the sentence once more, using new prepositional phrases. Repeat a third time, and a fourth. By now, they should be able to see the many possible variations.

Have students complete the exercise. You may wish to stop briefly after each sentence to discuss answers so that their skills are constantly being sharpened. Also check to be sure that the placement of the prepositional phrases has not altered the essential meaning of the sentence.

1. A gang war broke out in Chicago on December 3rd between the Tigers and the Rhinos.
2. He asked her to go diving for pearls off the Coral Reef in Australia on Valentine's Day.
3. Elizabeth and Michael climbed to the top of Pike's Peak for six hours in the rain on July 1st.
4. John wore new jeans of light green with the label of a rattlesnake on the back pocket.
5. Althea bought a small white elephant of porcelain with ivory tusks for $125.

C. (The information in this paragraph is true, taken from a newspaper account.) Have students complete the exercise. Check and discuss.

A Banana Olympics was held at Beloit College in Wisconsin in 1984. Ten teams competed in a banana-eating match, in a banana hunt, and in a Banana Punt, Pass, and Kick competition. One "fun" event was the Diving for Bananas Contest. The winner recovered 76 bananas in thirty seconds from the bottom of a swimming pool.

VARIATIONS AND FOLLOW-UPS

1. **Applying Their Knowledge.** Let the class work, as a group, at revising the paragraph in Exercise C. Suggest they add adjectives and adverbs and replace dull verbs with action verbs. Challenge them to develop an exciting, colorful account of the Banana Olympics.

2. **Game.** Divide the class into an even number of rows (4 or 6, for example). Have students in the odd-numbered rows (1, 3, 5) write a short sentence, e.g., The girl fell. Have the students in the even-numbered rows write an unusual or weird prepositional phrase, e.g., between two fish. Then have the students in rows 1 and 2, 3 and 4, 5 and 6 put sentences and phrases together, e.g., The girl fell between two fish. Repeat as often as you like. (This game may seem nonsensical, but it will etch on students' minds what a prepositional phrase is and how it fits into a sentence.)

STEP VI, Chapter 18, Purposeful Prepositions: Use Them in *Your* Writing!
Pages 93–95

A–E.   Have students complete the exercises. Check and discuss.

A.   Big Rock Candy Mountain is an imaginary land in the United States. With dogs that have rubber teeth and with jails made of tin, it is a favorite residence of tramps and hoboes.

B.   An unusual two-car collision occurred in Ohio in 1895 when the only two cars in the whole state managed to collide.

C.   Cockaigne is an imaginary land in France. People who love to eat live there on streets made of pastry and with stores that require no money from customers.

D.   An unusual wedding took place in Chicago in 1984. Inside a large cage, the bride and the groom, the clergyman, the best man, and the matron of honor participated, along with four Bengal tigers and three African lions. The bride said, "I'm a little nervous."

E.   A thief with a sweet tooth broke the front window of Schurra's Candy Factory in San Jose, California, just before Easter. The only thing stolen was a 40-pound, 3-foot-high chocolate bunny. Although the owner offered five pounds of jelly beans to anyone with information leading to the capture of the thief, the police as yet have no suspects and fear the culprit may have eaten the evidence.

Ten prepositional phrases were used.

Discuss WRITING TECHNIQUE 6 on page 95.

VARIATIONS AND FOLLOW-UPS

1. **Media.** The information in Exercises C, D, and E is true, taken from newspaper accounts. If your students enjoyed the material, suggest they browse through some newspapers and magazines to find unusual short items. Then have them develop similar exercises to try with each other. (This will motivate them to read and think, as well as to improve their skill with prepositional phrases.)

2. **Extending a Skill.** Explain that some words can be prepositions or conjunctions; the decision rests on the way the word is used. Write this pair of sentences on the chalkboard:

   Archie waited (until dinner). (prepositional phrase)
   Archie waited (until dinner was served). (dependent clause)

   Point out that in the first sentence, "until" is followed by a **noun,** forming a *prepositional phrase.* In the second sentence, "until" is followed by a **subject** and a **verb,** forming a *clause.* In the first sentence, "until" is a **preposition.** In the second, "until" is a **conjunction.**
   Have the students develop similar pairs of sentences for the following words.

   for   before   but

   (This will prepare students for later work on dependent clauses and emphasize the structure of prepositional phrases.)

3. **Extending a Skill.** Your students have already worked with pronouns, and now are familiar with prepositions. Point out that a pronoun following a preposition is in the **objective case.** Some examples should help them to see this clearly.

56

Ellie bought a lollipop (for him). (not "he")
Jerry talked (to her). (not "she")

So far, the use of the objective case is obvious. Now try this sentence.

Mario talked (to Max and _____). (I or me?) Tell them to omit "Max and"—Mario talked to ME. Obviously, "me" is correct and should also be used in the compound object.
Donald reserved tickets for (Gwen and _____). (I or me?) Omit "Gwen and"—and the answer is obviously "me."

A few more examples should solve this common problem and remove from the writing the erroneous use of "I" after a preposition.

WRITING—TIME II
Pages 96–100

Read the introductory material (page 96) aloud, pausing frequently to discuss the idea of "fleshing out" a sentence. After reading it, challenge the students to create a third Kris—and a fourth.

A. 1. Have students complete the exercise. Have several versions read aloud and discuss.

(a) chocolate fudge—large slab
(b) sailed; flew
(c) quickly
(d) her nephew—six years old
(e) warned

As the large slab of chocolate fudge cake sailed over her head, she ducked quickly. "Don't do that again," she warned her six-year-old nephew.

2. (a) five years old
(b) fifty cents
(c) for a soft ice cream
(d) begged

Five-year-old Lisa held out her hand. "Please give me fifty cents for a soft ice cream," she begged.

B. Have students complete the exercise. When they have finished, have several revised paragraphs read aloud. Encourage students to notice changes that really added power and vitality to the writing—or changes that turned the paragraph into a humorous item. Also— you may wish to remind them that writing is as distinctive as fingerprints: a person's style (use of words, structure of sentences) belongs to that one person alone.

After school, I started to walk home. I **craved** pizza—pizza **with pepperoni and sausage and peppers.** I **decided eagerly** to stop at **Roma's Pizza Parlor** and **devour** a couple of **juicy** slices. While I was **ambling lazily** along the street, I **spied** a **brand-new Cadillac fly** through the red light and **smash** into a 1961 VW. There was **the screaming of brakes, the screeching of metal, and the clattering of broken glass. The oversize owner** of the **oversize Cadillac jumped out** and started to **shout** at the **elderly lady who had been driving** the VW. **Furious at this injustice, I marched** over and told the driver of the **Cadillac** that I'd **witnessed** the whole thing. A police officer **arrived,** and I **reported** to her everything I'd witnessed. The **Cadillac owner bristled and fumed, but he couldn't deny it, for** I had seen it all. By the time everything was settled, it was far too late for my pizza.

Anecdote. Hemingway used mostly short, clipped sentences. At this point you may wish, to read a few sentences from one of Hemingway's short stories. These short, clipped sentences are a major factor in Hemingway's style. After he became famous, many writers tried to imitate his style—but all failed. Most good writers (and even some poor ones) have a clear-cut style that quickly identifies them. Tell your students that they are on their way to developing styles of their own. Help them to develop pride in their writing and to value the styles they are developing.

C. Have students complete the exercise. Versions of the "Fat Sparrow" story can be read and evaluated in class, or if you wish to use as a quiz, collect and grade with emphasis on the various techniques studied to date.

It was a rather ordinary day on September 5th, 1982, in a bank in Barcelona, Spain. People were making deposits and withdrawals, tellers were smiling—until a thief, known as The Fat Sparrow, carrying a cage of parakeets, strolled into the bank. Quickly he opened the door of the cage, and in moments parakeets were flying everywhere, zooming to the ceiling, bombing the heads of customers. Everyone—including the cashiers—jumped on to tables and counters, trying desperately to catch the panicked birds. Meanwhile The Fat Sparrow, armed with long-handled pincers, leisurely lifted bundles of banknotes from the cash drawer. Satisfied with his haul, he disappeared—leaving the parakeets and the disgruntled bank officials behind.

PREPARATION FOR UNIT TEST TWO (See test booklet.) For your convenience the answers appear on pp. 130–131 of this manual.

TEST PREPARATION

1. Review technical vocabulary: noun, verb, adjective, adverb, pronoun, preposition; generalization, details; general, specific; synonyms; alliteration; puns; revision; point of view; chronological, spatial.

2. Review briefly the three parts of speech studied earlier: noun, verb, adjective. Review the material following the procedure suggested on page 33.

3. Review thoroughly the three parts of speech just studied: adverb, pronoun, preposition. Practice by asking for:
   (a) adverbs that might describe a particular verb
      EXAMPLE: "scream"—loudly, desperately, harshly, etc.
   (b) prepositions (and prepositional phrases) that might follow a particular subject and verb

EXAMPLE: "The little girl hid her kitten"—under the couch; over the kitchen range; in the icebox, etc.
(c) pronouns that might be used in place of particular nouns
EXAMPLE: I offered my comic book to "Ellie." (her) "Jimmy" (he) offered his comic book to me.

4. Review with the students the difference between chronological and spatial organization. Ask:
   (a) Which would you use to describe the launching of a space vehicle? (chronological).

       List a few details for chronological organization:

       Astronauts enter space vehicle.
       Technicians check equipment.
       Rocket booster is fired.
   (b) Which would you use to describe a farm? (spatial)

       List a few details for spatial organization:

       Use the farmhouse as a central point.
       to the left is a barn.
       to the far left is a field of corn.
       to the rear are acres of vegetables: beans, tomatoes, etc.
       to the far right are apple orchards.
       to the near right is a garage.

Continue reviewing until students can grasp quickly the difference between chronological and spatial organization . . . and the way to develop each.

Introduce the Seventh Step to Better Writing—Four Types of Sentences: the declarative, the interrogative, the imperative, and the exclamatory. Call attention to the examples in the display box on page 102. Don't be too dismayed if your students are not familiar with these stars. You may wish to take a few moments to enlighten them about these movie greats and their careers.

UNIT THREE

STEP VII, Chapter 19, Four Types of Sentences: Learn Them!

Pages 102–107

A. Read together. Point out that declarative sentences, for the most part, make up the vast majority of the sentences we use. Have students complete the exercise. Check and discuss. (Answers will vary.)

B. Read together. Pay special attention to number 2: the rhetorical question. Emphasize the difference between a rhetorical question (one that does not require an answer) and a regular question (one that does). It may be helpful to have students complete (a), then check answers and discuss before going on to (b), etc.

    1. (Answers will vary.)

    2. (a) Should you buy a car next year—or now?
        (b) Why should you choose Sizzling Soda?
        (c) Is it fair to ask students to spend a full twelve months in school every year, when every adult in the country has at least a few weeks' vacation?
        (d) (Answers will vary.)

C–E. Read together. Have students complete the exercises. Check and discuss.

C. 1. Give that back to me.
    2. Get out of this house—and stay out.
    3. Cut out the nonsense and listen.

61

D. 1. Help!
   2. Not on your life!
   3. Fat chance!

E. 1. Get rid of that dog now.
   2. But Mom—he didn't know what he was doing.
   3. Won't you give him another chance?
   4. Never!

VARIATIONS AND FOLLOW-UPS

1. **Media.** As a homework assignment, ask students to watch TV or listen to the radio for fifteen minutes to identify the four types of sentences. They should write the examples, and note the sources: name of program; date; time; channel. Again mention that declarative sentences are most often used, but that the other three add variety and emphasis to both speaking and writing.

2. **Self-Knowledge.** Suggest students divide into small groups, each equipped with a tape recorder. Each group should tape a three-minute discussion. Some possible topics for discussion:

   > How should students who regularly disrupt a class be handled?
   > Should parents or teenagers have the final "say" about clothes?
   > Does a school have the right to order (or ban) a particular hairstyle?

   Do not tell them ahead of time the purpose of the taped discussions. After discussions have been completed, let each group play back the discussion, noting the types of sentences used by each participant. They should search for patterns. Does one student use mostly interrogative sentences? Another mostly imperative sentences? Finding the pattern is usually sufficient. Individuals can draw conclusions privately as to what the patterns suggest.

STEP VII, Chapter 20, Four Types of Sentences: Use Them!

Pages 108–112

A. Have students complete this exercise. Check and discuss. Remind them of correct punctuation.

1. Is the warthog the ugliest animal in the zoo?
2. The South Pole is covered with 8,850 feet of solid ice.
3. I won a million dollars in the lottery!
4. Will you please clean your room?
5. It would be helpful if you would list your talents below.
6. Send a check immediately.
7. I can't believe you mean it.
8. Doing homework at 5 A.M.!

B. 1. Read the Cooper quotation and paragraph together. Discuss, noting the use of three types of sentences for variety and emphasis. Have students work on the Ali quotation. Afterward, have several students read their paragraphs aloud and compare the various versions.

   Muhammad Ali once said, "No one knows what to say in the loser's room." What did the world-famous boxer mean? Ali, of course, knows all about the joyous clatter in the winner's room, but his comment suggests that he also knows all about the ominous silence in the loser's. In short, Ali knows the embarrassment, the humiliation felt by the loser and by the loser's friends. Clever Ali!

   2. Read the first three lines. Discuss the purpose of a formula in writing: to provide a plan for the writing of a varied interesting paragraph. Have students complete the exercise. Check and discuss.

   I have been accused of stealing five cents from the Candy Sale. I ask you—would I steal five cents? Of course I wouldn't! Such an accusation is clearly erroneous—and ridiculous, too.

3. Repeat the procedure used in 2.

"Walk twenty miles before dinner," my older sister ordered in a nasty tone of voice. I don't understand why big sisters think they can give orders—absurd orders, at that. Why should I obey? Walk the twenty miles yourself, sister dear!

C. Read together the introductory material. Read and discuss examples given. Emphasize the instructions to use two sentences, each of a different type. Have students complete number 1. Check and discuss. Then have students complete 2–6. Check and discuss.

1. My favorite entertainer is Jackie Gleason. Who wouldn't love that fat man who starred in *The Honeymooners*?
   (declarative + interrogative)
2. In my spare time I like to build huge castles of matchsticks. "You're crazy!" my mother declares.
   (declarative + exclamatory)
3. Why do I most want to visit Denmark? I want to see the storks and Tivoli Gardens and the friendly zoos and "The Little Mermaid" and a hundred other things.
   (interrogative + declarative)
4. Who would ever want to eat squash: mushy orange squash, or watery yellow squash, or even pulpy stringy acorn squash? Squash should be banned!
   (interrogative + exclamatory)
5. Which fictitious character do I most admire? My answer has to be—the handsome, swashbuckling, patriotic, powerful, suave, and gentle Rhett Butler in *Gone With the Wind*.
   (interrogative + declarative)
6. I am the middle child in a family of three children. That's an unfavorable situation!
   (declarative + exclamatory)

VARIATIONS AND FOLLOW-UPS

1. **Practice.** Have students in odd-numbered rows (Group 1) write declarative sentences, then hand them to students in even-numbered rows (Group 2). Have the second group of students add an

'exclamatory sentence that is logical or witty. This exercise can be repeated with variations:

Group 1: writing a rhetorical question
Group 2: writing a declarative sentence
Group 1: writing an imperative sentence
Group 2: writing a rhetorical question

2. **Tour de Force.** Challenge students to write a paragraph using imperative sentences plus one declarative sentence to conclude the paragraph. Follow the same procedure with interrogative sentences and exclamatory sentences.

EXAMPLE: Do your homework. Clean your room. Keep an eye on your little sister. Go to the store. Comb your hair. Sit up straight. Don't gulp your food. Commands, commands—that's all I hear from the time I get up until I go to bed.
(7 imperatives + 1 declarative)

STEP VII, Chapter 21, Four Types of Sentences: Use Them in *Your* Writing!
Pages 113–117

A. Have students complete parts 1, 2, and 3. Review briefly chronological and spatial organizations. Then read together the paragraph beginning with "You now have" and the sample paragraph. Discuss closely categorical organization. For practice, have students suggest three possible categories for each of the following topics:
(a) How teenagers spend their leisure time (sports; video games; parties)
(b) The grading system in our school (types of grades given; grades needed for sports participation; grades needed for promotion and graduation)
(c) This season's TV programming (comedies; dramas; music specials)
(d) Clothes and teenagers (buying clothes; bowing to peer pressure; parents' attitudes)

Now have students complete the exercise. Have several read aloud and evaluate.

B. Encourage the students to work independently. Check to see if they have grasped the concept of categorical organization. With less able students, begin with a discussion of possible categories of "Animals as Pets."

The categories used in the sample paragraph: dogs, horses, snakes.

Other possible categories:

Money-making pets: pedigree dogs; rabbits; ponies
Unusual pets: monkeys; parrots; cheetah cubs

Have students complete the exercise. Check and discuss.

C. This exercise is carefully planned, step by step. Students should have little difficulty with it if they follow the suggested procedure. Since it is a complete essay (suggested number of words: 200–250), you may wish to collect the final papers and grade them.

VARIATIONS AND FOLLOW-UPS

1. **Applying Their Knowledge.** Select a short story your students read recently, or one they read now. Afterward, have students work as a group to outline the story three times:

   chronologically
   spatially
   categorically

   Select the short story with care, or the spatial type of organization may be a problem. Two suitable stories:

   "The Most Dangerous Game" by Richard Connell
   "The Lottery" by Shirley Jackson

2. **Self-Knowledge.** Suggest that students apply categorical organization to their own lives. They've already worked with things they like, things they dislike, and things they fear. Now have them make up personal lists for the following:

problems they face (e.g., having a curfew)
type of people they admire (e.g., a recording artist)
school subjects (e.g., favorite subjects)
physical activities (e.g., walking to school)
mental activities (e.g., doing homework)
emotions they experience frequently (e.g., love)

These lists should be private, but suggest that the students study them in order to know themselves better.

Point out WRITING TECHNIQUE 7 on page 117. You may suggest that the students check their essays (Exercise 8) one more time to be sure they have a good variety of types of sentences.

STEP VIII, Chapter 22, Compound Sentences: Learn Them!
Pages 119–123

Introduce the Eighth Step to Better Writing—Compound Sentences. The students are probably familiar with the term, but this is an opportunity to demonstrate how compound sentences help to create a better flow of ideas when they are writing. Once again, you may wish to discuss the sources of the quotations in the display box.

Read the introductory material together. Discuss the word **compound** to be sure that the students understand it thoroughly.

A.   Have students complete the exercise. Check and discuss.

1.   shoplifter: one who lifts (steals) things from shops
2.   gumshoe: a rubber overshoe (a detective who moves quietly as though on rubber shoes)
3.   railroad: a road of parallel steel rails (used as a track for trains)
4.   skyscraper: a building so tall it seems to scrape the sky
5.   handkerchief: a hand kerchief; a kerchief to be held in the hand

B.   Read together the introductory material and the examples. As you do, have the students suggest additional sentences using compound subjects, verbs, etc. Have students complete this exercise. Check and discuss.

1. (Meg and Harley)—compound subject
2. (shrieked and whistled)—compound verb
3. (eardrums and patience)—compound object
4. (lifeguard and boss)—compound subject
   (reprimanded and banned)—compound verb
   (Meg and Harley)—compound object of "reprimanded"
   (beach and ocean)—compound object of "from"

C. Read together the introductory material. Emphasize that the three major coordinating conjunctions are **and, but, or.** Call the students' attention to the rule on page 122. You may also wish to elaborate on the use of the plus, minus, and equal signs. Have students complete the exercise. Check and discuss.

1. and
2. but
3. or

VARIATIONS AND FOLLOW-UPS

1. **Extending Their Knowledge.** Compound words are fascinating, and an awareness of their parts strengthens our appreciation of our language. Suggest that the students compile a long list of compound words, using both dictionaries and their memories. Have them star their favorites. Some possibilities:

catfish	bookworm	windbag	rowboat
clodhopper	killjoy	bullfrog	greenhorn
bluegrass	grapevine	tenderfoot	letterhead

2. **Writing.** Ask each student to select one compound word and research its origin. Emphasize here the value of the OED (Oxford English Dictionary). Most libraries will have a copy of at least the two-volume compact edition. Suggest they collect everything they can about the chosen word. (Other sources: specific references, e.g., for "catfish," a book about fish; for "greenhorn," a book about the West; books of word origins; other dictionaries.)

   When they have enough information, have the students write a paragraph about the word. They may include the meaning, the origin, the earliest use, various usages, and any other relevant information. Remind them to use various types of sentences and to organize chronologically, spatially, or categorically.

Revised paragraphs can be combined into a booklet for their own use or for the school library.

3. **Vocabulary.** Review the various meanings of **compound:**

> compound a felony (verb)
> compound fracture (adjective)
> compound interest (adjective)
> compound subjects (adjective)
> compound verbs (adjective)
> compound objects (adjective)
> compound sentences
>   Add:
> compound (noun) — a fenced or walled-in area containing buildings (animal compound; native compound; compound for humans in game preserve; also used with prisons, military forces, concentration camps, etc.).

STEP VIII, Chapter 23, Compound Sentences: Use Them!
Pages 124–127

A. Work on Exercise 1 together. Discuss. Emphasize the need for a comma before the coordinating conjunction. Then have students complete the exercise. Check and discuss.

1. During their shopping expedition, Don bought three video game cartridges, and Jan bought six LP records.
2. I have been a pilot for five years, but I have never flown across the Atlantic Ocean.
3. Are you going to call Jason, or shall I?
4. The teacher lectured, but most of the students didn't take notes.
5. Ellen likes baseball, and her brother Tom likes football, but their sister Sue doesn't like any sports.

B. Work on Exercise 1 together. Have as many read aloud as time permits, both to check accuracy of work and to provide reinforcement. In Exercise 2, point out that "alternative" means offering a choice of plans or methods. Have students complete the exercise. Check and discuss.

1. I am exceedingly fond of ice cream, and I like cookies almost as much.
2. I would spend the $50,000 on computer equipment, or I would spend it on a trip around the world.
3. I would like to live in Switzerland, but I would miss my family and friends.
4. I would love to visit the moon, but unfortunately I have a fear of heights.
5. Robins herald the spring, and snow showers warn that winter is on its way.
6. I would like to sail a boat, and I would like to develop a fine stamp collection.
7. I would like to accept your invitation to participate in an African safari, but I hope you are offering a guarantee against attacks by elephants and tigers.
8. Dogs make loyal and fun-loving pets, but tropical fish couldn't care less about their owners.
9. I am willing to wash cars and even shampoo upholstery, but I absolutely refuse to polish chrome.
10. Josie will carry the scientific equipment, Lauren will carry the cooking equipment, and Jennifer will carry the provisions.

C. Point out that "vitality" means liveliness, animation—qualities the students would like their writing to possess. Students should aim for vitality as they work independently on this exercise. Read the original version aloud. Have several students read aloud their revised versions. Compare for smoothness and interest.

Cliff went for a hike, and Mac went with him. They walked briskly along West Mountain Road for about two hours. They were tired, but they were not exhausted. They decided to climb Googol Mountain, but they didn't quite make it to the top. As it grew dark, they trudged home, their legs aching and their feet blistered.

70

VARIATIONS AND FOLLOW-UPS

1. **Practice.** Have one student suggest a topic and then have other students volunteer a compound sentence on that topic. Continue as long as student interest lasts.

2. **Practice.** Challenge students to write a . . .
   compound declarative sentence
   compound interrogative sentence
   compound imperative sentence

3. **Vocabulary.** Review meanings of . . .
   undulating (wavelike) (page 124)
   coordinating (connecting) (page 122)
   conjunction (word that connects two words or clauses) (page 122)

   Ask students to write sentences using the words. Have a few read aloud to reinforce learning.

STEP VIII, Chapter 24, Compound Sentences: Use Them in *Your* Writing!
Pages 128–131

A. Talk about "fillers"—what they are, why they are used. Bring to class and read aloud a few fillers from a recent newspaper.

   The word "incorporate" is used later on page 128. Point out that "incorporate" is a verb meaning "to combine into a united whole."

   Have students complete the exercise. Later, ask several students to read their versions aloud. Discuss the quality of writing in each and suggest that other students compare theirs with the ones read.

   Why do we shake hands to greet someone? Why not touch feet instead, or rub noses, or even bump heads? There's a perfectly good reason. In ancient times most males carried weapons, and men who didn't know each other well were wary when they met. They hesitated to get too close, since one might draw a knife or a sword and

71

stab the other. So it became a custom for both men to put down their weapons and extend empty hands to show good faith. Soon the empty hands clasped, and the handshake was born.

B. For some students, several words may need explanation.

> originated = began
> vendors = sellers, especially street sellers
> dachshund = small dog with long body, short legs, and droopy ears

Have students complete the exercise. Check and discuss.

C. Have students complete the exercise. Check and discuss.

VARIATIONS AND FOLLOW-UPS

1. Vocabulary. Review meanings of . . .

> filler (noun) (page 128)
> incorporate (verb) (page 128)
> originated (verb) (page 129)
> vendors (noun) (page 129)
> dachshund (noun) (page 129)

Be sure the students understand the five words . . . but especially "filler," which will be used in later lessons.

2. Punctuation. Explain that sometimes a compound sentence is formed by combining two sentences with a semicolon rather than with a conjunction.

EXAMPLE: Mary fed the giraffes and sheep; Louise, braver by far, fed the tigers and hyenas.

The sentence could use the conjunction **and,** but because there are other **ands** in the sentence, a semicolon is preferable.

Ask students to suggest similar compound sentences using the semicolon. Remind them that a semicolon = a comma **plus** a coordinating conjunction.

3. **Game.** Write the clauses in Column 2 below on the chalkboard. Read one clause from Column 1 (*not* in order) and ask the students to select the clause from Column 2 that best completes the proverb.

Column 1	Column 2
Spare the rod,	but you cannot make him drink.
A fool may make money,	and repent in leisure.
Marry in haste,	and spoil the child.
You can lead a horse to water,	but only one to start it.
A wise man changes his mind,	but it requires a wise man to
It takes two to make a	spend it.
quarrel,	and time makes love pass away.
Love makes time pass away,	but a fool never.

This exercise should help to emphasize the close relationship between the two parts of a compound sentence.

4. **Writing.** Have students select one of the proverbs in Exercise 3, think about it, and explain it briefly.

Point out WRITING TECHNIQUE 8 on page 131. This may be a good time to review WRITING TECHNIQUES 1–8 before launching into complex-sentence structure.

STEP IX, Chapter 25, Complex Sentences: Learn Them!

Pages 133–137

Introduce the Ninth Step to Better Writing—Complex Sentences. Discuss what is meant by one part of a sentence being dependent on another. Point out the use of complex sentences in the display box.

A. Read the introductory material (pages 134–135) aloud and discuss at length. Make sure the idea of "complex" is clear to your students. Have students complete the exercise. Have several dependent clauses read aloud to check accuracy and to reinforce learning.

1. Millicent hit a homer **because** she wanted to prove that she could.
2. Everyone will vote for you for class president **if** you distribute pizza at lunch time.
3. Four-year-old Timmy smashed his tricycle **when** he ran into the concrete wall.
4. Max devoured two whole pizzas **although** he had just finished a huge turkey dinner.
5. I'll have a banana split **after** we finish the sundaes.

B. Read the introductory material together. Have students complete the exercise. Check and discuss. Point out that the placement of the dependent clause should depend on the whole sentence. The most important part of the sentence should come last. In sentence 1, for example, "I will give you a million dollars" should probably come last. In sentence 2, if the dependent clause is "When she received a dime," the main clause should probably come last. But if the dependent clause changed to "When she saw the little purple man from Mars"—then the order probably should be reversed: "She jumped for joy when she saw the little purple man from Mars."

Point out that in the above paragraph the word *probably* is used frequently because there is seldom one right answer for *where* a dependent clause should be placed. Placement depends (1) on the relative importance of the two parts of a complex sentence, and (2) on the rhythm of the writing in the paragraph in which the complex sentence is a part.

1. **If** you walk the full length of the Great Wall of China, I will give you a million dollars.
2. **When** she won the election, she jumped for joy.
3. The automobile, **after** it collided with the oil truck, was a total wreck.
4. The monster, **before** it gobbled up its victim, smiled sweetly.
5. **Because** you destroyed the computer deliberately, you will be grounded for three months.

C. Have students complete this exercise. Check and discuss.

1. (<u>If</u> you win the lottery)
2. (<u>when</u> he came face to face with a grizzly bear)

74

'3. (<u>although</u> Cari had studied nonstop for 72 hours)
4. (<u>after</u> it bit the cow)
5. (<u>until</u> he met one)

Point out the rules for using the comma (page 136). Have students locate the commas in the sentences that are referenced here.

D. Make this a "fun exercise." Read the introductory material aloud. Explain that clues to combining the right dependent clauses and main clauses lie in meaning, in vocabulary, and in tone. Have students complete the exercise. Check and discuss.

1. If you haven't got charity in your heart,
2. where an individual has the opportunity to go from nothing to something.
3. unless he's Humphrey Bogart.
4. when I was three and unknown.
5. until they can be made unbreakable.
6. that people will look at anything rather than each other.
7. If someone is dumb enough to offer me a million dollars to make a picture,
8. who said talk is cheap?

VARIATIONS AND FOLLOW-UPS

1. **Practice.** Consider the eight sentences in Exercise D. Ask students to rearrange the clause placement.

Sentence 1: "If you haven't got charity in your heart, you have the worst kind of heart trouble."

Rearrange to read:

"You have the worst kind of heart trouble if you haven't got charity in your heart."

Is one arrangement clearly better than another? (In regard to sentence 1, either arrangement is possible, but the first version is stronger.)

Sentence 2: Changing the two clauses would make an awkward sentence. Only one arrangement is satisfactory.

Sentence 3:   Here the two clauses could be switched, but placing the dependent clause at the beginning would sharply lessen the dramatic impact of the sentence.

Continue with sentences 4–8.

2.   **Vocabulary.** Review the meanings of:
   (a)   clause (a group of words having a subject and a verb)
   (b)   independent clause (a clause that can stand alone)
   (c)   dependent clause (a clause that depends on another clause)
   (d)   dependent (basic meaning: a person or thing that cannot exist without the help of another) Children are dependent on their parents or other authorities. Invalids are dependent. We all, when we are seriously ill, are dependent on doctors for help.
   (e)   complex (basic meaning: consisting of interconnected parts) In grammar, one or more of the interconnected parts are dependent on another. "Complexion" includes texture, appearance, and color tint of the facial skin.

3.   **Punctuation.** Remind students that when a dependent clause appears at the beginning of a sentence, it is followed by a comma. When a dependent clause appears at the end of a sentence, usually no comma is required. Have the students suggest ten or twelve complex sentences. Write them on the chalkboard. Emphasize correct punctuation.

STEP IX, Chapter 26, Complex Sentences: Use Them!

Pages 138–143

Explain the difference between **coordinate** and **subordinate** conjunctions. Have the students refer to the rules on page 138.

A.   Use Exercises 1 and 2 orally with the students as a group. Remind them to choose the exact subordinate conjunction required to show the relationship between the independent and the dependent clauses—and to place second, the clause they think is most important. Students should then be able to handle Exercises 3 through 10 individually. Check and discuss.

1. When the hunter spotted the deer, he raised his rifle.
2. Before she started up the Matterhorn, she checked over her mountain-climbing equipment.
3. Because her pet alligator died, she cried for weeks.
4. Soaring across the sky in a hot-air balloon is a fascinating experience that you should try.
5. While I was watching a terrifying star wars movie, an explosion rocked the house.
6. When Frank lost his ball, he plunged into a snowdrift to find it although he had no mittens or hat or jacket.
7. When the Martian smiled, the Earthling trembled because she knew the alien planned to kidnap her.
8. After I foolishly left the main road, I found myself in a swamp that was full of alligators and mammoth mosquitoes.
9. The toddlers' world consists mostly of adults who tower above them and must seem like giants.
10. The petrel is a seabird that appears to be walking on water when it flies along the tops of waves.

B. Read the introductory material together. Encourage students to be funny—even silly—in creating the dependent clauses. Work on Exercise 1 orally, and ask for many suggestions . . .

When the fly sat on my head, I cried bitterly.

I cried bitterly because my pet mosquitoes had an argument.

Have students complete the exercise. Check and discuss.

1. **When I broke my shoelace,** I cried bitterly.
2. **As he hid the sheets behind the TV,** Edwin laughed gleefully.
3. **Because I did not study,** I cannot answer.
4. **If you do not work hard,** you will fail.
5. **Because he pulled her pigtail,** Brenda slapped him.
6. I won't go **unless Jason and Melissa go, too.**
7. **When there is a full moon,** Daniel is moody.
8. **When her escort did not bring her a corsage,** Lilybell pouted.
9. **When the play was over,** Oliver collapsed.
10. **After the bullfight was over,** the spectators applauded.

C. Have students complete the exercise. Direct them to tackle the exercise step by step. When they have finished, point out that all sorts of complex material (instructions for putting a bike together, for example) can be handled if they follow instructions step by step rather than trying to absorb all the steps at one time. When they have finished, read the original paragraph aloud, and then have two or three students read aloud their revised paragraphs. Encourage the class to compare the different versions and to see the difference made by sentence structure and vocabulary.

VARIATIONS AND FOLLOW-UPS

1. **Practice.** To reinforce learning and to emphasize how dependent clauses affect the meaning of a sentence, let students create a few dependent clause "fans." (For prepositional phrase fans, see page 83.)

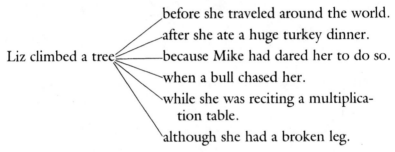

Liz climbed a tree
before she traveled around the world.
after she ate a huge turkey dinner.
because Mike had dared her to do so.
when a bull chased her.
while she was reciting a multiplication table.
although she had a broken leg.

Continue with other key sentences as long as the exercise seems profitable.

2. **Spelling.** Since subordinate conjunctions are often misspelled, give students the following list and ask them to memorize the spelling of each word. Advise them that only a perfect score will be acceptable.

after	although	because	as
if	since	that	unless
until	when	where	which
while	why		

Point out that "until" has only one "l." Point out that "when," "where," "which," "while," and "why" all start with a "wh."

STEP IX, Chapter 27, Complex Sentences: Use Them in *Your* Writing!
Pages 144–147

A. Teenagers love books of records and facts. You may wish to cash in on this interest by borrowing from the school library some of the most popular reference books of this type.
Some possibilities:

Guinness Book of World Records (Norris McWhirter)
The Women's Book of World Records and Achievements (Lois O'Neill)
The Ethnic Almanac (Stephanie Bernardo)
The U.S. Fact Book (Bureau of Census)
The World Almanac & Book of Facts (Newspaper Enterprises)
The Hammond Almanac (KNX/CBS Newsradio 1070)
The People's Almanac (Wallechinsky and Wallace) (three volumes)

Try to find at least *four* reference books of this type. Divide students into four groups, giving each group one reference book to browse through. Then have them exchange books. Do this two more times until all groups have checked all four reference books. (Suggest that, as they browse, they make notes of any especially fascinating information they come across, including the source.)

Now have them proceed with Exercise A. Collect the paragraphs, read rapidly, and select a few to be typed and/or reproduced. Have students read and discuss:
(a) methods of organization
(b) use of several types of sentences
(c) use of strong nouns, verbs, adjectives, and adverbs
(d) general effectiveness

B. Read the first four sentences aloud. Discuss the phrase "tour de force." Have students complete the exercise. Check and discuss. (Answers will vary.)

C. Most students should be able to handle this exercise with no help. With less able students, read the first question (What is the name of this park?). Discuss. Have each student make a decision and write down the chosen name. Continue with question 2, etc.

Next have the students read the letters they wrote on page 44. Point out the major parts of a friendly letter.

Now have them proceed with Exercise B. When they have finished, ask them to put a check in the margin next to each complex sentence.

Later, either read and discuss their letters, or collect for grading. Discuss WRITING TECHNIQUE 9 on page 147.

VARIATIONS AND FOLLOW-UPS

1. **Vocabulary.** Review meanings of:

    tour de force (act of great skill, strength, or ingenuity—page 145)
    input (information fed into a computer or human brain—page 146)
    format (size, shape, and general makeup of a letter or a printed page—page 30)

    Discuss words. Have students use them in sentences.

2. **Game.** Write on the chalkboard the clauses in Column 2 below. Read one clause from Column 1 (*not* in order) and ask the students to select a clause from Column 2 that will complete the proverb correctly. Then ask them to state which of the two clauses is the main clause and which is the dependent clause. Ask them to identify the subordinate conjunction. Repeat this procedure with each of the proverbs.

Column 1	Column 2
A fool can ask questions	that wise men cannot answer.
When the cat's away,	the mice will play.
As the twig is bent,	the tree's inclined.
It is too late to lock the stable door	after the horse is stolen.
Make hay	while the sun shines.
While there's life,	there's hope.
Where ignorance is bliss,	'tis folly to be wise.
As you make your bed,	so must you lie in it.
Strike	while the iron is hot.
Practice	what you preach.
Preachers can talk but never teach	unless they practice what they preach.
Fools rush in	where angels fear to tread.
If at first you don't succeed,	try, try again.
Never count your chickens	before they're hatched.
Never put off until tomorrow	what you can do today.
If wishes were horses,	beggars would ride.

This exercise should help to emphasize the close relationship between the two parts of a complex sentence . . . and will, at the same time, review the structure of a complex sentence and the use of the subordinate conjunction.

3. **Writing.** Have students select one of the proverbs in Exercise 2, think about it, and explain it briefly.

WRITING TIME—III
Pages 148–151

A. In Writing Time II, students "fleshed out" single sentences. Now they are being asked to flesh out a sentence and follow it with an exciting paragraph. Read together the introductory material on page 148. Most students should be able to proceed with the exercise. Less able students may need guidance. You may need to discuss the meaning of *scenario* with the students.

B. Have students complete exercise. Check and discuss.

   Tons of water cascaded into white foam, and the roar stunned the ears of Jerry Greene and his wife, Catherine. It was their first visit to Niagara Falls, New York, and there was nothing remotely like this in Boise, Idaho, their hometown. A little later, the Greenes were stunned again, this time unpleasantly; for Jerry's wallet was missing, and in it was $10,000—all the money the Greenes owned. Two years passed, and they lost all hope that they would ever recover their money. Then, a few days ago, ten-year-old Ellie Drew was playing in the tall grass on the Three Sisters, a tiny island near the Falls. Ellie found Greene's wallet and quickly returned it to him. For the Greenes, it was a doubly joyful occasion: they had their money back, and they had found an honest child. For Ellie, it was joyful, too—she now had a $200 reward to spend in any way she liked.

C. Have students complete the exercise. Have a few revisions read aloud. Ask the other students to listen and to compare with their own revisions. Discuss.

PREPARATION FOR UNIT TEST THREE. (See test booklet.) For your convenience the answers to the test appear on pp. 132–133 of this manual.

TEST PREPARATION

1. Review technical vocabulary.

    Parts of speech: noun, verb, adjective, adverb, pronoun, preposition, conjunction

    Methods of organization: chronological, spatial, categorical, general to specific details, generalization

    Aids to good writing: synonyms, alliteration, puns, revision

    Point of View

    Types of sentences: declarative, interrogative, imperative, exclamatory

    Terms: tour de force, rhetorical question

    Types of sentence structure: compound, complex

    Types of conjunctions: coordinate conjunction, subordinate conjunction

2. Review thoroughly the parts of speech using the procedures outlined on pages 33 and 42.

3. Review thoroughly the four types of sentences. An easy way to do this is to have the students compose a paragraph orally.

    Ask student 1 to compose a declarative sentence.

    Ask student 2 to follow with an interrogative sentence that might logically follow sentence 1.

    Ask student 3 to follow with a declarative sentence that might logically follow sentence 2.

    Ask student 4 to follow with an imperative sentence that might logically follow sentence 3, etc.

4. Review thoroughly the compound sentence. Give a topic and ask for a compound sentence about it.

EXAMPLE: Doing dishes: My brother washed the dinner dishes, and I dried them.

EXAMPLE: Recognizing trees: Jeremy recognized the red maple, but I wasn't able to.

5. Review thoroughly the complex sentence. Give a topic and ask for a complex sentence about it.

EXAMPLE: Climbing a mountain: Billy climbed until he reached the peak of the mountain.

EXAMPLE: Driving a car: The doctor drove rapidly because he was overdue at the hospital.

UNIT FOUR

STEP X, Chapter 28, Appositives: Learn Them!
Pages 153–158

The Tenth Step to Better Writing—Appositives—is introduced on page 153. Read the introduction to this unit aloud. Point out the words in apposition in the display box. Ask the students to suggest other similiar ads that use a product name plus a descriptive phrase. In this way they will get the "feel" of the appositive before beginning the exercises.

A. 1. Read together the introductory material on page 154. Then begin exercise 1 working as a group. After students have completed sentence 1(a), check the answer. Then ask—does it matter which comes first: the noun or the descriptive phrase? (Yes, it does. The most important element comes first, usually the noun.) Point out the difference between:

Mandarin, China's national language, is spoken by 726 million people. (emphasis on "Mandarin")
and
China's national language, Mandarin, is spoken by 726 million people. (emphasis on "China's national language")

Have students complete the exercise. Check and discuss.

(a) China's national language—arrow to "Mandarin"
(b) English—arrow to "The major language of the Western world"
(c) the fiftieth state to be admitted to the Union—arrow to "Hawaii"
(d) a miserly millionaire—arrow to "Hetty Green"
(e) the wildly imaginative inventor and cartoonist—arrow to "Rube Goldberg"

2. Have students complete the exercise. Repeat the procedure used in Exercise 1.

(a) the fear of cats—arrow to "ailurophobia"
(b) a llamalike animal of the Andes—arrow to "vicuna"
(c) tropical grass with hollow woody stems—arrow to "bamboo"
(d) a new electronic-age language—arrow to "Logo"
(e) a bacon, lettuce, and tomato sandwich—arrow to "BLT"

3. Have students complete the exercise. Repeat the procedure used in Exercise 1.

(a) a colorful contraption designed to amuse babies—arrow to "cradle gym"
(b) a platinum blonde—arrow to "Maryanne"
(c) a corn-growing state—arrow to "Iowa"
(d) a tall, six-foot redhead—arrow to "Giovanni"
(e) a prison for princes—arrow to "Tower of London"

B. Have students complete the exercise. Check and discuss.

1. a popular drink in Old England / an adjective now used to describe the gown and the ceremony
2. preferably the English classroom / the study of language, especially of the Greek and Latin languages / uneducated people who were often superstitious
3. a young man and a young woman / usually Italian or Spanish or French
4. usually the wife but sometimes the husband / actually "eating money"
5. a month-long period of happiness / a brief period right after the election when almost everyone admires him

VARIATIONS AND FOLLOW-UPS

1. **Vocabulary.** If students enjoyed Exercise B, assign a word to each of the students and have them find the origin of the word and use it in a sentence, including an appositive. Some possibilities:

ambulance	omelet	ostracize	pinafore
dandelion	petrel	planet	oleomargarine
pawn	salary	penthouse	robot
pretzel	racketeer	sandwich	prevaricate
rival	schlemiel	tennis	sophomore

2. **Vocabulary.** If students seem to enjoy finding out the origin of words, challenge them to find the origin of:

> their state name
> their county name
> their town or city name

The first should be easy, the last two possibly more difficult. You might add to the list:

> street names that have specific origins
> sections of the town or the city
> nicknames (if any)

3. **Practice.** To provide students with additional practice in writing appositives, write on the chalkboard a list of ten current celebrities. Ask the students to create a descriptive appositive for each. Afterward, have them compare and evaluate their work.

STEP X, Chapter 29, Appositives: Use Them!
Pages 159–164

A. Read the introductory material together. Point out that in the "baboon" example, the two sentences *can* be combined by "and" into a compound sentence. However, combining them by using an appositive results in a smoother, more compact sentence. Have students complete the exercise. After every two or three sentences, stop and have the students read their answers. Discuss; then have the students continue the work.

1. James Buchanan, the only bachelor to serve as President of the United States, was elected in 1856.
2. Philadelphia, the city of "Brotherly Love," owes its name to the Greek word "philos," which means "love," and to the Greek word "adelphos," which means "brother."
3. Beethoven, a world-famous musician, composed most of his great symphonies after he became deaf.
4. Rats, carriers of disease, have probably been responsible for more deaths than all the wars of history.

5. The Empire State Building, the second largest building in New York City, was made with ten million bricks.

Read and discuss the example on page 160. Point out how the commas are used to set off the appositives.

6. James Madison, the fourth President of the United States, was also the smallest. Madison, a Virginian, was only 5 feet 4 inches tall and weighed less than one hundred pounds.

7. In the Midwest in the 1880s, some towns forbade the sale of ice cream sodas on Sunday, the Lord's Day. A clever store owner skipped the soda and served a "Sunday soda," just ice cream and syrup. Eventually the name was shortened to "sundae."

8. The chewing gum that has been around the longest is Black Jack, a licorice-flavored gum. Another interesting gum, a sour-pickle-flavored concoction, is mildly popular in Japan.

9. Bob Hope, one of the most popular people in show business, was once a prizefighter. Desi Arnaz, a successful actor-director, was once a cleaner of bird cages.

10. Failure isn't permanent. John F. Kennedy, the popular thirty-fifth President of the United States, lost by a landslide when he ran for president of his freshman class. Lucille Ball, the much-loved star of the "I Love Lucy" series, was told she had no acting ability when she applied to a drama school.

B. Encourage students to create interesting, amusing, and provocative appositives. They will enjoy the work more and will also enjoy exchanging answers.

1. a paradise for surfboarders and microchip technicians
2. an ancient actress with a fierce temper
3. chocolate cake with three scoops of ice cream, chocolate sauce, and whipped cream
4. the ant-eating aardvark
5. taking pictures in the Adirondack Mountains
6. silent sentinels that almost scrape the sky
7. an undersize recruit with an oversize confidence
8. winner of this year's Frog Beauty Contest
9. a shower of red, white, and gold
10. the six-o'clock news broadcast

C. Less able students may need words such as guru, lair, and orbs defined before beginning the exercise. Have them complete the exercise and read several revisions aloud.

My brother, a four-year-old electronic game champ, twiddles the joysticks as though he had been doing it for twenty years. Like a miniature guru, he sits cross-legged in front of our TV set, the lair of dozens of exciting games. He inserts his favorite cartridge, *Asteroids*. His eyes, gleaming orbs of anticipation, glitter. He starts to play, gleefully manipulating the joysticks, twin tools to bliss. Five hours later he has racked up a fine score, a million points. My mother comes home, turns off the TV, and pulls the joysticks from his small, numb hands. "Enough, Einstein," she says firmly as she picks him up. "It's time for your nap."

Discuss the value of appositives:
(a) to make sentences more compact
(b) to make sentences more "meaty"
(c) to make sentences smoother

VARIATIONS AND FOLLOW-UPS

1. **Research.** If you wish to offer your students some research work combined with practice using appositives, try this assignment.
(A) Use any library reference to find the following:
    (1) an interesting fact about one U.S. President
    (2) the nickname of your state
    (3) one interesting fact about your state
    (4) one interesting fact about one animal
    (5) one interesting fact about one bird

    (Especially useful will be almanacs, books of records, and "first facts" books.)
(B) Use the reference material to:
    (1) Write two sentences about each of the five items above. (Be sure that the two sentences can be combined by turning one into an appositive.) Write these ten sentences on one side of a sheet of paper.
    (2) Combine the sentences in each of the five groups into one sentence, using an appositive. Write the resulting five sentences on the reverse side of the paper.

(C) Bring papers to class.
  (1) Exchange papers and have each student combine someone else's five pairs of sentences.

  or

  (2) Collect and prepare several sheets of two-sentence clusters for the students to combine, using appositives. They'll enjoy this exercise more if you place the initials of the contributing student in parentheses after each cluster.

2. **Punctuation.** Point out that an appositive is separated from the rest of the sentence by two commas, one before it and one after it, if the appositive falls within the sentence, and by one comma if the appositive ends the sentence.

   Use the sentences developed in (C) above as an exercise in punctuation.

3. **Media.** Have students browse through magazines and newspapers to find five examples of appositives. If possible, these should be clipped and pasted on a sheet of paper. Display the sheets on the bulletin board or tape them to the frame of the chalkboard and let students wander around the room, reading and discussing some of the appositives.

STEP X, Chapter 30, Appositives: Use Them in *Your* Writing!
Pages 165–171

A. 1. Read the assignment and the example together. Ask the students to jot down on a piece of scrap paper three people who changed their lives. (Some students may need help. Suggestions: a teacher, a doctor, a clergyperson, a parent, a friend.) Have students complete the exercise. Check and discuss. (Answers will vary.)

'2. Follow the same procedure as in Exercise I. (Suggestions if needed: cities, monuments, museums, festivals, etc.)

3. Follow the same procedure as in Exercise 1. (Suggestions if needed: success in school, on a job, in sports, in hobbies, etc.)

B. Before students begin this exercise, spend a few minutes discussing *contrast*. Ask them to contrast (orally):

(a) two very different cars
(b) two books or movies
(c) two kinds of trees (or flowers or stores, etc.)

With the concept of *contrast* grasped, they should have little difficulty with the assignment. Have students complete the exercise. Check and discuss. (Answers will vary.)

C. Read together the introductory material and the sample paragraph. Discuss the two aspects—comparison/contrast—until the students understand them clearly. Have them provide details orally for a comparison/contrast of:

(a) two sports
(b) two snack foods
(c) two kinds of dancing

1. Now that they have grasped the difference between comparison and contrast, they should be able to complete Exercise 1. Have several read aloud; discuss and evaluate.

2. Repeat the procedure used in Exercise I. Instead of having paragraphs read aloud, you may prefer to collect them for grading. If you do, emphasize the use of appositives and the development of comparison/contrast.

VARIATIONS AND FOLLOW-UPS

1. **Media.** Have students check old newspapers (the library should have a file of them) to find an editorial or a feature column that compares and contrasts two things or people or systems. (If possible,

they should choose something about a local issue or problem.) Then, working in groups, have them select two that are well written and lively. Make copies of the articles, or use an opaque projector so that all students can examine the writing simultaneously.

Analyze the articles for:

(a) use of comparison: similarities
(b) use of contrast: differences
(c) drawing of a conclusion
(d) use of strong nouns, verbs, adjectives, and adverbs
(e) use of varied types of sentences and sentence structures
(f) use of appositives

2. **Writing.** After students have completed Exercise I above, ask them to plan and organize an editorial or a feature column of their own. Some possible topics:

My mother's (or father's) life as a youth
My favorite school subject—and my least favorite
Mothers and fathers
Parents and grandparents
The recording artists of yesterday—and the recording artists of today

Planning and organizing should include:

(a) a title
(b) a list of similarities
(c) a list of differences
(d) a decision as to which items of (b) and (c) should be used second, third, or fourth, and which should be discarded.

When the students have completed planning and organizing, they should then write an editorial or a feature column, using the above information and outline. Suggest that they follow one of the models studied in Exercise 1. Remind them to use the various writing techniques they have been studying. Discuss WRITING TECHNIQUE 10 on page 171.

STEP XI, Chapter 31, Parallel Structure: Learn It!

Pages 173–178

PREPARATION

On the chalkboard use a ruler to draw several sets of parallel lines. The sets should be drawn horizontally, vertically, and diagonally. Point out that although parallel lines may be of all lengths and may go in all directions, they never meet—they continue an equal distance apart.

Words, phrases, sentences, and even paragraphs may be parallel. Parallel structure is a useful technique in writing.

Read aloud the introduction to the Eleventh Step to Better Writing—Parallel Structure on page 173. Identify the parallel structures in the sentences in the display box. Help the students to understand the order, clarity, and rhythm that parallel structure gives to writing.

Point out the grammatical structures that should be paired as presented on page 174.

A. Be sure students understand the concept of parallel structure in writing: the use of similar structures, one following another.

    1. Do (a), (b) and (c) aloud. Then have the students work on (d) through (j). Check and discuss.

        (a) gardening
        (b) embezzlement
        (c) brute force
        (d) Collecting wooden nickels
        (e) hated by his enemies
        (f) brief
        (g) to go to sleep
        (h) how to read
        (i) by the flashing of lights
        (j) charismatic

B. Have students complete this exercise. Check and discuss.

    1. intrigued—fascinated—obsessed
    2. in . . . headland—in . . . beach—in . . . sand

3. urns and . . . busts—cherubs—alligators—a peacock; sit—toot—double—spreads
4. if . . . wins—if . . . loses
5. to love—to feel

C. Some students should be able to work successfully on this exercise without further help. Others may need assistance to grasp the idea behind the exercise. If they do, ask them questions such as:

1. To bake a cake, you should . . . (Give three instructions, each starting with a verb or an infinitive.)

   Add $\frac{1}{2}$ cup of butter.
   Beat for two minutes.
   Pour into greased pan.

2. I like holidays . . . (Give three reasons, each beginning with the subordinate conjunction "because.")

   because we have good things to eat,
   because we usually have company, and
   because we don't have to go to school.

Continue making up base sentences and letting students complete them using parallel structure. When they seem comfortable using parallel structure, have them complete Exercise C. Check and discuss.

1. to buy pizza, and to help their families.
2. should mark all prices clearly, and should offer frequent sales.
3. drought, with frequent dust storms, and blizzards, with heavy snow and sweeping winds.
4. good health, and a long life.
5. Abraham Lincoln because he was compassionate and had a conscience, and John Fitzgerald Kennedy because he brought hope to millions of people.
6. I enjoyed reading . . .
   Gone With the Wind because it is a romantic epic about the Civil War,

The Yearling because it is a touching story about a boy and a deer, and

Kon-Tiki because it tells how a man crossed the ocean on a balsa raft.

7. Teenagers run away from home . . .
   because they are physically abused,
   because they have had an argument with their parents, or
   because they are seeking adventure.

8. City streets are sometimes dangerous because of . . .
   muggers,
   fast-moving traffic, and
   con artists.

9. Country roads are sometimes dangerous because of . . .
   wild bulls,
   nipping geese, and
   flash floods.

10. Automobile accidents are caused by . . .
    sleepy drivers,
    icy roads, and
    illegal speeds.

VARIATIONS AND FOLLOW-UPS

1. **Vocabulary.** Review meanings of:

   infinitive (to + a verb) (page 174)

   gerund (verb form used as a noun and ending in "—ing" or "—ed" (page 174)

   parallel structure (parallel parts of a sentence or of a paragraph should be similar in structure)

   Review the three terms with the students. Ask them to provide several sentences using infinitives, gerunds, and parallel structure.

2. **Practice and Review.** Make this an opportunity to provide additional practice in using parallel structure and to provide a review of the various aspects of grammar already studied.

Instructions:

(a) Write a sentence using infinitives in parallel structure.
(b) Write a sentence using gerunds in parallel structure.
(c) Write a sentence using nouns in parallel structure.
(d) Write a sentence using verbs in parallel structure.
(e) Write a sentence using prepositional phrases in parallel structure.
(f) Write a sentence using dependent clauses in parallel structure.
(g) Write three declarative sentences, employing parallel structure.
(h) Write three imperative sentences, employing parallel structure.
(i) Write three interrogative sentences, employing parallel structure.
(j) Write one compound sentence, using three main clauses and employing parallel structure.

Dictate each instruction and have students write a sentence to the pattern. Check and discuss. Or you may wish to write each of the ten instructions on small pieces of paper. Ask for ten volunteers to take part in a parallel structure "bee." Pull one instruction from a hat or box, read it, and have student 1 provide a suitable sentence. If student 1 is successful, proceed to student 2 and a second question. If student 1 is not successful, he or she sits down and is out of the game. Instructions can be reused until most—or all—of the students have been counted out.

STEP XI, Chapter 32, Parallel Structure: Use It
Pages 179–184

Read the introductory material with your class.

A. Work on Exercise 1 together. Have many "recipes" suggested; discuss each. Then work on Exercise 2 together. Again—have many sentences suggested and discuss each. Students should then be able to complete Exercises 3 through 5. Check and discuss.

B. These five exercises are distinctly different. Your students will be most successful if you tackle them one at a time. Let students discuss how to do Exercise 1; have them do it; check and discuss. Continue using the same procedure for Exercises 2 through 5.

1. (a) daring
   (b) cautious
   (c) ambitious

2 through 5. (Answers will vary.)

C. Read the introductory material (pages 182–183 to "Now it's your turn . . .") together. Discuss each revision carefully. Read aloud the original paragraph and the revised paragraph. Emphasize the difference made by thoughtful revision. Then challenge students to revise the "electronic-game arcade paragraph," using many of the same techniques. When they have finished, read the original paragraph aloud and have several students read their revised paragraphs aloud. Discuss the difference made by the revisions.

Spending a day in an electronic-game arcade is fun. I can spend hours playing my favorites: *Asteroids*, *Pac-Man*, and *Moon Patrol*. Who wouldn't love an arcade? All around me are flashing lights, piercing whistles, thunderous booms, and shrieking players. Time passes on greased wheels as I control the universe. Exciting, dynamic, breathtaking, this place makes my blood race and my heart pound. It makes me feel alive.

VARIATIONS AND FOLLOW-UPS

1. **Media.** Ask the students to browse through newspapers and magazines, looking for good examples of parallel structure. Have them bring these to class and share the best ones.

2. **Speeches.** Ask the students to examine speeches by political figures, past and present. As they skim the speeches, they should look for good examples of parallel structure. (Some of the best sources: Franklin D. Roosevelt; John Fitzgerald Kennedy; Winston Churchill; Abraham Lincoln; Thomas Jefferson.) Have each student bring

one or two examples to class for discussion. Ask: Why have the very best speakers so often used parallel structure? (Sentences "build" on each other, culminating in a powerful impact on the listener.)

3. **Writing.** Ask the students to think of something each would like to "sell." It might be a particular brand of soft drink; it might be a candidate running for class president; it might be an idea, for example, teenagers should (or should not) have a curfew. Then ask them to write a paragraph that would be part of a speech. The paragraph should include a strong example of parallel structure. You may wish to point out that ads usually use short sentences and phrases to do a selling job, whereas political speakers usually use longer sentences and phrases—the first because they want a quick immediate impact, the second because they want to give a sense of force and power. When the students have finished, have a few read aloud. Discuss and evaluate.

STEP XI, Chapter 33, Parallel Structure: Use It in *Your* Writing!
Pages 185–190

A. Work on Exercise 1 orally. Let students suggest phrases to fill the two blanks. Select the two best, insert them, and read the paragraph aloud. Then have the students work on Exercise 2 individually. Check and discuss.

1. rusty screws and bent nails
   marbles, bottle caps, and bits of string.
2. (Answers will vary.)

B. Work on Exercise 1 orally. Let students suggest clauses to fill the two blanks. Select the two best, insert them, and read the paragraph aloud. Then have the students work on Exercise 2 individually. Check and discuss.

1. promise longer free periods and no homework;
   have free ice cream every day
2. (Answers will vary.)

C. Most students should be able to follow the step-by-step procedure outlined for writing an essay. Some may need help, especially in the earlier stages. Help can probably be given best on a one-to-one basis. You may wish to collect these essays for grading. If you like, give two grades: one overall grade and one specifically for use of parallel structure.

VARIATIONS AND FOLLOW-UPS

1. **Revision.** Bring to class copies of a newspaper article that is rather dull. Distribute copies; ask students to revise the article, using all the techniques already studied, but with special emphasis on parallel structure. Or divide the class into small groups and let each group work on a revision. Later, have several of the best revisions read to the class as a whole. Discuss the fact that words and the arrangement of words make a difference.

2. **Game.** Just for fun (and to reinforce learning) ask all students to write an infinitive clause on a piece of scrap paper. (EXAMPLE: to sit for hours on a brick wall.) Ask three students to read their clauses aloud and write these on the chalkboard, putting a comma after the first and second, and an "and" before the third. Then preface with a base sentence such as—"I really like . . ." Have someone read the complete sentence aloud, probably to peals of laughter. Repeat, using:

   > parallel gerund phrases (fighting in the school yard)
   > (Base sentence to follow the gerund phrases: ". . . are my favorite activities.")
   > parallel prepositional phrases (in the stagnant waters of the Lazy River)
   > (Base sentence to precede the prepositional phrases: "My friends and I enjoy lolling . . .")

   Add as many more instructions and base sentences as you like. Discuss WRITING TECHNIQUE 11 on page 190.

STEP XII, Chapter 34, Verbals: Learn Them!
Pages 192–199

Introduce the Twelfth Step to Better Writing—Verbals.
Students are awed by verbals—and therefore afraid of them. Overcome this fear by making this chapter especially enjoyable. Read page 192 aloud. (We've tried to give you a head start by using PIGS as the theme.)

A. Emphasize the two clues to recognizing a participle: that it is formed by adding "—ing" or "—ed" to a verb, and that it is used as an adjective. Read the four examples with your students. Then work with them on Exercise 1(a). Check and discuss. Continue the procedure through 1(b)–(e) and 2. Before the students tackle Exercise 3, ask orally for suggestions of participles or participial phrases used in sentences. When they seem at ease with participles, have them complete Exercise 3. Check and discuss.

1. (a) dancing—arrow to "pig"
   (b) exhausted—arrow to "marathoners"
   (c) hog-calling—arrow to "contests"
   (d) flying—arrow to "machine"
   (e) worried—arrow to "Sal"
2. (a) measuring six feet in length—arrow to "Borean Pig"
   (b) nicknamed "Fred's Pigs"—arrow to "piglets"
   (c) biting more savagely than a tiger—arrow to "boar"
   (d) frightened by the huge waves—arrow to "Allie"
   (e) panting for air—arrow to "Eddie"
3. (Answers will vary.)

B. Read the introductory material together. Point out that infinitives are easy to recognize (to + a verb); but that they are used in various ways.

1. Have students complete Exercise 1. Check and discuss.

   (a) to play
   (b) to sing
   (c) to sleep
   (d) to fly
   (e) to win

2. Read the introductory material together. After reading each sentence used as an example, ask students to create PIG participial phrases that would work in the sentence. (EXAMPLES: *To eat like a pig* is a no-no. I was too happy *to want to be a pig.* Her plan *to permit pigs in school* was unpopular.) Have students complete the exercise. Check and discuss.

    (a)   to relax with a chocolate sundae
    (b)   to fetch a newspaper—to pull a cart—to play the piano
    (c)   to jump off the Brooklyn Bridge
    (d)   to talk about it
    (e)   to try it again

3. Again—just for fun—challenge students to use all five infinitives in sentences about PIGS. Check and discuss.

C. Students find gerunds the most difficult of the three types of verbals. Emphasize that the gerund is used as a noun and may be the subject of a verb or the object of a verb or of a preposition.

1. Have students complete the exercise. Check and discuss.

    (a)   talking
    (b)   skiing
    (c)   dancing
    (d)   hiking
    (e)   thinking—writing

2. Read the introductory material together. After reading each sentence used as an example, ask the students to create PIG gerund phrases that would work in the sentence. (EXAMPLES: *Teaching a pig to eat neatly* is a waste of time. I appreciate your *helping me to build a pigsty.* The man was arrested *for kidnaping a 500-pound pig.*)

    (a)   golfing with his friends
    (b)   using motorized roller skates
    (c)   learning to fly
    (d)   flapping its wings furiously
    (e)   acting like an adult

3. Again—just for fun—challenge the students to use all five gerunds in sentences about PIGS. Check and discuss.

VARIATIONS AND FOLLOW-UPS

1. **Vocabulary.** Review meanings of:
   (a) *participle* (verbal formed by adding "—ing" or "—ed" to a verb; used as an adjective)
   (b) *infinitive* (verbal formed by using "to" + a verb)
   (c) *gerund* (verbal formed by adding "—ing" to a verb; used as a noun)
   (d) *panorama* (a broad presentation of a subject; may be visual or verbal)
   (e) *infrangible* (cannot be broken or separated into parts)
   (f) *genuine* (real, true, honest)

   Discuss. Have students use the terms in original sentences.

2. **Game.** For a review of the three verbals, have one student challenge another.

   Give me a sentence about _____ . Include a (an)

   _____ .

   The first blank may be filled by any NOUN. The second blank should be filled with an INFINITIVE, a GERUND, or a PARTICIPAL.

   EXAMPLE: Give me a sentence about **robots**. Include an INFINITIVE.
   ANSWER: I am going *to build* a robot that will mow our lawn.

   Continue until all three verbals have been used several times.

3. **GAME.** To review grammar already studied and to show how a sentence can be developed, try this game. Provide a base sentence:

   We will play . . .

   Ask student 1 to provide a noun as an object.

   We will play tennis.

   Ask student 2 to add a prepositional phrase.

   We will play tennis for three hours daily.

Ask student 3 to add an infinitive or an infinitive phrase.

> We will play tennis for three hours daily to strengthen our leg muscles.

Ask student 4 to add a participal or a participial phrase.

> We will play tennis for three hours daily to strengthen our weakened leg muscles.

Ask student 5 to add a gerund or a gerund phrase.

> As part of our training for the tournament, we will play tennis for three hours daily to strengthen our weakened leg muscles.

Other base sentences and development:

> Andrew proved his skill . . .

Ask student 1 to add a prepositional phrase.

> Andrew proved his skill in football.

Ask student 2 to add a gerund or a gerund phrase.

> Andrew proved his skill in football by kicking a ball 60 yards.

Ask student 3 to add an appositive.

> Andrew, a 100-pound lightweight, proved his skill in football by kicking a ball 60 yards.

Ask student 4 to add an infinitive or an infinitive phrase.

> To win a position on the team, Andrew, a 100-pound lightweight, proved his skill in football by kicking a ball 60 yards.

Ask student 5 to add a participle or a participial phrase.

> To win a position on the team, Andrew, a 100-pound lightweight, proved his newly acquired skill in football by kicking a ball 60 yards.

Base sentence: Melissa wrote . . .

Ask student 1 to add a noun used as the object of the verb "wrote."

> Melissa wrote a novel. . .

Ask student 2 to add a prepositional phrase.

Melissa wrote a novel about pigs.

Ask student 3 to add an infinitive or an infinitive phrase.

To earn money, Melissa wrote a novel about pigs.

Ask student 4 to add a participle or a participial phrase.

To earn money, Melissa wrote a blistering novel about pigs.

Ask student 5 to add a gerund or a gerund phrase.

To earn money for surfing, Melissa wrote a blistering novel about pigs.

Ask student 6 to add an appositive.

To earn money for surfing, her favorite hobby, Melissa wrote a blistering novel about pigs.

For additional practice add as many base sentences as you like.

STEP XII, Chapter 35, Verbals: Use Them!
Pages 200–205

Before students begin working on this chapter, have them turn to the cartoon on page 202. Read the caption aloud, letting the students enjoy the absurd situation created by a misplaced modifier. Then turn back to page 200.

A. Read the introductory material aloud, emphasizing the various methods that can be used to correct sentences with misplaced modifiers. Work as a group on sentences 1 and 2. Then have students correct sentences 3–11. Check and discuss.

   1. The streets in the sixteenth century were kept clear of waste food by the pigs acting as a sort of sanitation department.
   2. A farmer needs only a well-fed sow to produce a litter of eight to ten healthy piglets twice a year.
   3. Jobs are guaranteed for all graduates who go to the institute for two years.
   4. We watched the antics of the monkeys playing inside the cage.

5. To win the contest, you must write a four-line jingle about pigs.
6. Before visiting Washington, D.C., one should study maps and carefully check guidebooks.
7. As I stood on the street corner, a truck smashed me to the ground.
8. Riding in a hansom cab, we reveled in the beauty and serenity of Central Park.
9. After enduring sleet, hailstones, and hurricane winds, we found the haystack a welcome refuge.
10. To be eligible for the first prize, you must submit three box tops with the entry.

B. Ask for volunteers to do 1 and 2 orally, emphasizing the need to place the modifiers correctly. Have students work on items 3–7 independently. Check and discuss.

1. A female pig or hog is called a *sow*, rhyming with *cow*.
2. In 1863 in Cincinnati, then called "Porkopolis," over 600,000 hogs were slaughtered.
3. Pigs often wallow in mud to cool themselves off.
4. Picking up letters written on cards and arranging them enabled the "Learned Pig" in London in 1789 to write words.
5. Charles Braverman of Chicago collects pig memorabilia, including a $2,000 brass pig dinner bell and a $2,400 pig ashtray.
6. In 1776 salt pork was smuggled past British sentries at night to provide food for Washington's troops at Valley Forge.
7. Finding a trained pig is difficult because most pigs don't go to school.

C. Read aloud the story about pigs. Ask the students to analyze what is wrong with it. (Short sentences; no variety in type or length of sentence; dull verbs.) Then challenge them to revise the story, using the suggestions in (a), (b) and (c) in addition to all their writing skills. Afterward, have one or more students read the revised stories aloud. Point out how revision increased the smoothness and rhythm of the writing, the interest level, and the readability.

In the millions of years pigs have been around, they have changed little. They still have forty-four teeth, fourteen ribs, and cloven

105

hooves. They are round and shortlegged with a thick skin covered with short, coarse bristles. Pigs have long snouts and small curly tails. They carry their heads low, eat and drink close to the ground, and breathe close to the ground, too. Some are white with black on their faces and legs, and some are red. Some have white spots on a black background, and a few are black and have a white belt around the body. Centuries ago, pigs were used as scavengers to keep the streets clean. Today they provide pork, a popular food, bacon, and sausages. Pigs eat everything: potatoes and artichokes, snakes and birds. They even eat earthworms, insects, and nuts. A New England farmer once said, "Dogs look up to you, cats look down on you, and pigs think you're their equal." Pigs are fascinating animals.

VARIATIONS AND FOLLOW-UPS

1. **Practice.** If you have three or four students who can draw fairly well, divide your class into small groups, each including one "artist." Ask the other members of the group to create absurd sentences using misplaced modifiers. The "artist" in the groups should then draw cartoons illustrating these absurdities. Next, have the groups exchange papers and correct misplaced modifiers. These papers can be displayed on a bulletin board.

2. **Media.** Ask students to scour the classified ads of the local newspapers to spot misplaced modifiers (and any other grammatical errors). They should clip these and paste them on a sheet of paper. Later, in class, discuss each ad and rewrite, emphasizing that correct grammar adds clarity and appeal. These ads, too, with the revisions can be posted on the bulletin board. You can use this exercise to teach students how to read a classified ad. Write some of the common abbreviations on the chalkboard and discuss what they stand for and why they are used.

3. **Writing.** Have each student write at least one classified ad. Tell the students the result should be an ad that is grammatically correct and has sales appeal.

4. **Review.** (first or last five minutes of class) Mention one at a time various aspects of grammar studied so far. Have volunteers define each term. Encourage competition and fast thinking.

noun	participle
pronoun	adverb
imperative sentence	declarative sentence
appositive	compound sentence
gerund	verbals
adjective	verb
preposition	interrogative sentence
exclamatory sentence	complex sentence
parallel structure	infinitive

STEP XII, Chapter 36, Verbals: Use Them in *Your* Writing!
Pages 206–209

A. Have students complete the exercise. Check and discuss.

1. to dance, to play on a seesaw, to climb a ladder, to balance balls on their snouts, and to write words
2. burrowing, burrowing, containing, having, to jump, to give birth

B. You may wish (especially with less able students) to permit students to work on this exercise in small groups. In fact, this will be a good time to introduce them to the concept of "brainstorming." Suggest that each group begin by dreaming up an unusual pig. Students should share their ideas, even silly ones, allowing these ideas to trigger still more ideas. One student should take brief notes. After a few minutes, call a halt to the brainstorming and ask each group to consider the ideas presented and to select "its" pig. The same procedure will work for choosing a name for the pig.

Group work should be effective in this exercise, since brainstorming often stirs even sluggish imaginations. Later, each group can choose a spokesperson to present its pig and TV show to the class. After all reports have been made, let the class vote to choose the TV show that would have the greatest chance for success with a general audience and the one that would have the greatest chance of success with small children.

C. This assignment will be handled best by students working individually. Make sure all students understand the assignment, then have them proceed. The assignment may be completed in two class periods, or in one homework assignment (making notes and organizing) and one class period (for the actual writing). You may wish to collect papers and grade as a writing exercise.

VARIATIONS AND FOLLOW-UPS

1. **Media.** (follow-up of Exercise B) Suggest that students become PR (public relations) people for "their" pig and TV show. Ask them to provide, in writing:
   (a) a brief bio of their pig—one suitable for release to a newspaper or magazine
   (b) an ad selling the new TV show—one suitable for the local newspaper
   (c) a paragraph suggesting additional ways of "using" their pig to make money (e.g., on T-shirts)

   Remind them that they are writing "professionally" and their writing should be clever and amusing.

2. **Revision.** (follow-up of Exercise 1 above) When students have completed the assignment outlined in the exercise above, have them exchange papers. Each student (or group) should study carefully the other's work and suggest revisions that would improve it. Have papers and suggestions returned. Now have each student (or group) revise the work incorporating all or some of the suggestions. Spend a little class time discussing revision and what it can accomplish.

3. **Review.** (first or last five minutes of period) Mention one at a time the various aspects of grammar so far studied. Ask for volunteers (or call on students) to provide an example of each.
   Point out WRITING TECHNIQUE 12. You may wish to have students read aloud the WRITING TECHNIQUE for each of the examples given in Exercise 3 above.

STEP XIII, Chapter 37, Combining Sentences: Nursery Level

Pages 211–215

The Thirteenth Step to Better Writing—Sentence Combining—is introduced on page 211. Have the students compare the two examples in the display box.

PREPARATION

Read the introductory material aloud. Enjoy with your students the richness and flexibility of our language that allows us to rearrange the same words in so many different ways. (Review the meaning of *tour de force*.)

A. Work on this exercise as a group. Students should compete enthusiastically as they try to find twelve combinations. Write suggested sentences on the chalkboard. (If they have trouble, offer clues: How about starting with a prepositional phrase? How about using an appositive? etc.)

1. The cow jumped over the moon, and the little dog laughed.
2. When the cow jumped over the moon, the little dog laughed.
3. When it jumped over the moon, the cow made the little dog laugh.
4. Jumping over the moon, the cow made the little dog laugh.
5. The little dog laughed as the cow jumped over the moon.
6. The little dog laughed at the cow jumping over the moon.
7. The cow, jumping over the moon, made the little dog laugh.
8. Over the moon the cow jumped, making the little dog laugh.
9. Over the moon jumped the cow, making the little dog laugh.
10. Because the cow jumped over the moon, the little dog laughed.
11. The little dog laughed at the cow, which had jumped over the moon.
12. To make the little dog laugh, the cow jumped over the moon.

B. Have students complete the exercise. Check and discuss.

1. Little Tommy Tucker sang for his supper: brown bread and butter.
2. For a supper of brown bread and butter, Little Tommy Tucker sang.
3. Little Tommy Tucker sang to get brown bread and butter for his supper.
4. By singing, Little Tommy Tucker earned a supper of brown bread and butter.
5. A supper of brown bread and butter was Little Tommy Tucker's reward for singing.

C. Have students complete the exercise. Check and discuss.

1. Little Bo Peep has lost her sheep, and she doesn't know where to find them.
2. Little Bo Peep doesn't know where to find the sheep that she lost.
3. Little Bo Peep's sheep are lost, and she doesn't know where to find them.
4. Her sheep lost, Little Bo Peep doesn't know where to find them.
5. After losing her sheep, Little Bo Peep doesn't know where to find them.

D. Have students complete the exercise. Check and discuss.

1. Jack and Jill went up the hill to fetch a pail of water.
2. To fetch a pail of water, Jack and Jill went up the hill.
3. Up the hill went Jack and Jill to fetch a pail of water.
4. Jack and Jill, to fetch a pail of water, went up the hill.
5. Wanting to fetch a pail of water, Jack and Jill went up the hill.

VARIATIONS AND FOLLOW-UPS

1. **Game.** Offer extra credit (or any suitable reward) to any student who can create two sentences that can be combined in at least twelve ways. To prove this, the student should write the two base sentences on the chalkboard and then accept suggested sentence combinations from the other students. (These should also be written on the board.)

2. **Punctuation.** Using the twelve sentences developed in Exercise 1, review some of the rules for use of the comma:

> A comma is used after a dependent clause that appears at the beginning of a sentence.
> Commas are placed before and after dependent clauses that appear in the middle of a sentence.
> Commas are placed before and after appositives.
> A comma is usually placed after a prepositional phrase that appears at the beginning of a sentence.
> A comma is placed after a participial phrase that appears at the beginning of a sentence.

Point out that a comma indicates a pause and is used primarily to insure clarity of meaning.

3. **Analysis.** Write on the chalkboard this nursery rhyme.

> Little Jack Horner sat in the corner,
> Eating his Christmas pie.
> He stuck in a thumb and pulled out a plum
> And said: "What a good boy am I!"

This nursery rhyme is made up of two sentences. Ask:

Sentence 1: What is the subject of the main clause? (Jack Horner)

What is the verb of the main clause? (sat)
What adjective describes Jack? (little)
Identify a prepositional phrase. (in the corner)
Identify a participial phrase. (eating his Christmas pie)
Where *should* the participial phrase be located? (immediately after Jack Horner)
Find a personal pronoun. (his)

Sentence 2: What is the subject of the main clause? (He)

What verbs are found in the predicate? (stuck . . . pulled . . . said)
What are the prepositions? (in . . . out)
What bit of dialogue is used? ("What a good boy am I!")
Now ask these additional questions or give the following instructions:

111

(a) Combine the two sentences into one. (As Little Jack Horner . . .)
(b) Break into five short sentences.
(c) Why did the author write, "What a good boy am I!" rather than "What a good boy I am!"? (to rhyme with pie; for smoothness)
(d) If the author had used "I am" instead of "am I," how could the second line be changed to rhyme properly? (eating his Christmas ham)
(e) Following (d), what changes would have to be made in line 3? (Something like—he plucked with his thumb and extracted a crumb.)
(f) Suggest a stronger verb for "eating" (gulping) and for "said" (cried).

STEP XIII, Chapter 38, Combining Sentences: Junior Level

Pages 216–217

A. There are ten clusters of sentences in this exercise. Have students complete the first five. Then check and discuss. Have them complete the second five. Check and discuss. (The discussion after the first five will help those who are still having difficulty combining sentences.)

1. The first Martian appeared on Sunday, March 1st, while everybody was in church.
2. As three tramps invaded our tiny town, the dogs all began barking madly.
3. It was cold and dark as Dana slipped out of the house at midnight.
4. Max likes Mackintosh apples, big, juicy oranges, and cherries.
5. Joyce Ann swims every day in the Olympic-size Community Pool.
6. For the forty million dogs in the United States, two billion dollars is spent every year on dog food.
7. A slanted line, called a *virgule*, sometimes divides dates and choices (4/4/84; he/she).

8. Every year Americans devour about 200,000 tons of popcorn, much of it in movie theaters.
9. Paul Bunyan had a blue ox called Babe that measured 42 axe handles, and a plug of chewing tobacco between its horns.
10. Tennis was born in France in the fifteenth century when nobles, batting a cloth ball back and forth, often shouted "Tenez," which means "Take it."

VARIATIONS AND FOLLOW-UPS

1. **Analysis.** Follow the procedure given in **VARIATIONS AND FOLLOW-UPS,** Exercise 3 of Chapter 37 (page 109) with this nursery rhyme.

> Old Mother Hubbard went to the cupboard
>   To get her poor doggie a bone.
> But when she got there, the cupboard was bare,
>   And so her poor doggie got none.

2. **Writing.** Rewrite "Old Mother Hubbard" in prose. Make it as exciting and as dramatic as you can. Use strong forceful verbs. Use apt adjectives. Vary sentence structure.

3. **Media.** Distribute a class set of the local newspaper (or photo copies of a short newspaper story).

> First: Have students analyze the story, identifying various sentence structures.
> Second: Ask the students to combine some sentences and to break up others. (Do these changes increase or decrease the effectiveness of the writing?)
> Third: Ask the students if any verbs can be replaced by stronger verbs, or any general nouns by specific nouns.
> Fourth: Evaluate the original version. Does it need improvement, or is it good as it stands? Have the students make a decision and support it.

Pages 218–222

(All information in the following sentences is true.)
Have students work on each cluster. Check and discuss.

1. Gene Tunney, a heavyweight boxing champion, also lectured on Shakespeare at Yale University.

2. Sergei Prokofiev, a Russian composer, composed an opera when he was seven years old. This opera, "The Giant," used only the white keys on the piano.

3. In 1891, Whitcomb L. Judson, a Chicago inventor, took out a patent for the zipper. Meaning for it to replace buttons on shoes, he called it the "Clasp Locker and Unlocker for Shoes."

4. In 1904, Richard Blechynden, an Englishman, sold tea at the St. Louis World's Fair. One intolerably hot day nobody wanted hot tea. Blechynden tried serving it cold. The result? Iced tea!

5. St. Patrick was actually British. He saw Ireland for the first time when he was kidnapped by some Irishmen. After he escaped, he became a priest, then a bishop, and finally a missionary. When he went back to Ireland, he was highly successful in his missionary work there. He became the patron saint of Ireland.

6. Rudyard Kipling, the author of *The Jungle Books* and *Kim*, lived in Brattleboro, Vermont, for five years. Kipling liked outdoor exercise even in winter. In Vermont it snows almost constantly during the winter, so Kipling invented snow golf. He painted the balls red so that he could locate them in the snow.

7. In 1845 the population of Ireland was 8.25 million. In 1848 Ireland was struck by a devastating potato famine, and by 1851 the population was down to 6.50 million. About one million had died, and about one million had emigrated.

8. James Barry joined the medical corps of the army of Queen Victoria. After serving as a surgeon for forty years, he eventually was promoted to inspector-general of hospitals. In 1865 he died. After his death, it was discovered that "he" was a "she," for Barry was a woman who had successfully masqueraded as a man for over forty years!

9. Four friends vacationing in Switzerland agreed that each would write a ghost story. The poets, Shelley and Byron, never finished theirs, nor did Dr. John Polidori. But Mary Wollstonecraft Godwin did. She was eighteen and the wife of Percy Shelley. That ghost story, published two years later in 1818, was called *Frankenstein*.

10. The Brothers Grimm wrote about two hundred fairy tales in which males and females are not exactly equal. There are sixteen wicked mothers or stepmothers and only three wicked fathers or stepfathers; twenty-three evil female witches and only two evil male witches; thirteen young women who endanger men and only one man who harms his bride.

VARIATIONS AND FOLLOW-UPS

1. **Practice.** Write the following sentences on the chalkboard:

   This happened 87 years ago. Our ancestors started a nation on this continent. This nation was to give liberty to everyone. It was to support the idea that all people are equal.

   Ask students to combine the four sentences into one, making any changes they like in vocabulary or arrangement of words but *not* in information.

   When they have finished, have a few read aloud. Then show them how Abraham Lincoln wrote the sentence. Point out that the four dull sentences—through good writing—become one powerful ringing sentence.

   Fourscore and seven years ago our fathers brought forth upon this continent a new nation, conceived in liberty and dedicated to the proposition that all men are created equal.

You should point out that Lincoln wrote five different versions of this famous speech.

2. **Analysis.** On page 117 is a copy of "The Gettysburg Address" by Abraham Lincoln (November 19, 1863). Make photocopies and distribute them to the students. Read the address aloud, emphasizing the powerful rolling rhythm—the significant pauses—the memorable phrasing. Next, ask the students to analyze the writing.

    Some possible approaches:

    (a) Prepositional phrases: (1: upon this continent) (1: in liberty) (1: to the proposition)

    (b) Participles and participial phrases: (1: dedicated . . .) (2: testing . . .)

    (c) Parallel Structure: (1: conceived . . . dedicated . . .) (10: of the people, by the people, and for the people) (6: we cannot dedicate, we cannot consecrate, we cannot hallow . . .)

    (d) Appositives: (9: the living)

    (e) Dependent clauses: (1: that all men . . . equal) (4: that that nation . . . live) (5: that we . . . this)

    (f) Adjectives: (1: new) (2: great, civil) (3: great) (10: great) (10: new) (Notice probably deliberate repetition of two adjectives, "new" and "great.")

    (g) Infinitives: (4: to dedicate) (7: to add or detract)

    (h) Count number of words in each sentence. (1: 30; 2: 24; 3: 10; 4: 27; 5: 11; 6: 16; 7: 22; 8: 21; 9: 22; 10: 34) Draw attention to the two short sentences (3 and 5) and to the extremely long one (10). But sentence 10, while long, is divided—through the use of parallel dependent clauses—into four related but distinct thoughts.

THE GETTYSBURG ADDRESS
by Abraham Lincoln

[1]Fourscore and seven years ago our fathers brought forth upon this continent a new nation, conceived in Liberty and dedicated to the proposition that all men are created equal.

[2]Now we are engaged in a great civil war, testing whether that nation, or any nation so conceived and so dedicated, can long endure.

[3]We are met on a great battlefield of that war.

[4]We have come to dedicate a portion of that field, as a final resting-place of those who here gave their lives that that nation might live.

[5]It is altogether fitting and proper that we should do this.

[6]But, in a larger sense we cannot dedicate—we cannot consecrate—we cannot hallow—this ground.

[7]The brave men, living and dead, who struggled here, have consecrated it far above our poor power to add or detract.

[8]The world will little note, nor long remember, what we say here, but it can never forget what they did here.

[9]It is for us the living, rather, to be dedicated here to the unfinished work they have thus far so nobly advanced.

[10]It is rather for us to be here dedicated to the great task remaining before us—that from these honored dead we take increased devotion to that cause for which they here gave the last full measure of devotion—that we here highly resolve that these dead shall not have died in vain—that this nation, under God, shall have a new birth of freedom—and that government of the people, by the people, and for the people shall not perish from the earth.

STEP XIII, Chapter 40, Combining Sentences: Use Them in *Your* Writing!

Pages 223–225

Some students may need help with steps 1 and 2. After that, all students should be able to complete this exercise successfully. Tell them that the assignment will be fairly easy *if* they take it step by step.

This assignment will probably take two days. When the students have finished, collect papers and grade.

Call attention to the final WRITING TECHNIQUE on page 225. See how many students can recall all thirteen techniques. Reward them with a generous round of applause.

WRITING—TIME IV

Pages 226–231

A. Have students complete the exercise. Check and discuss.

> Twelve-year-old Sean tossed his books into the closet and slammed the door. School was over at last! For ten glorious weeks, he could spend hours in a darkened theater, transported to a world of adventure and daring. Or he could ride the waves on his surfboard, or practice his powerful breaststroke in the cool waters of the Atlantic. He could run, or leap, or climb trees. He could, if he felt like it, just lie in the grass and dream. He was free! For ten glorious weeks, he was free!

> I threw my books in the closet and slammed the door. School was over at last! For ten glorious weeks, I could spend hours in a darkened theater, transported to a world of adventure and daring. Or I could ride the waves on my surfboard, or practice my powerful breaststroke in the cool waters of the Atlantic. I could run, or leap, or climb trees. I could, if I felt like it, just lie in the grass and dream. I was free! For ten glorious weeks, I was free!

B. After the students have completed this exercise, have them move into small groups to read and evaluate their stories. (Answers will vary.)

C. You may wish to collect this essay to grade as a writing assignment. This is a very personal essay; you can increase student satisfaction by writing a few humorous or quizzical comments about their choices and wording.

PREPARATION FOR UNIT TEST IV (See test booklet.) For your convenience the answers appear on pp. 134–135 of this manual.

TEST PREPARATION

1. Review of technical vocabulary.

   > *Parts of speech:* noun, verb, adjective, adverb, pronoun, preposition, conjunction
   >
   > *Methods of organization:* chronological, spatial, categorical, general to specific, details, generalization
   >
   > *Aids to good writing:* synonyms, alliteration, puns, revision
   >
   > *Point of View*
   >
   > *Types of Sentences:* declarative, interrogative, imperative, exclamatory
   >
   > *Terms: tour de force,* rhetorical question
   > *Types of Sentence Structure:* compound, complex
   >
   > *Types of Conjunctions:* coordinate conjunction, subordinate conjunction

2. Review thoroughly the parts of speech, using the procedures outlined on pages 33 and 59 of this manual.

3. Review the four types of sentences, using the procedure outlined on page 83.

4. Review compound and complex sentences. (See pages 83–84.)

5. Review appositives. Use comic-strip characters in brief sentences. Ask students to insert a suitable appositive.

EXAMPLE: Mickey Mouse is the star of Disneyland.
Mickey Mouse, the world's most clever rodent, is the star of Disneyland.

EXAMPLE: Veronica is the spoiled daughter of a millionaire.
Veronica, Archie's girl friend, is the spoiled daughter of a millionaire.

6. Review parallel structure. Give the students a base sentence. Ask them to complete the base sentence using parallel structure.

EXAMPLE: I read a newspaper daily in order . . .

to learn what is happening in the world,
to discover the sports scores, and
to laugh at the comics.

EXAMPLE: Many teenagers like to ride motorcycles because . .

they are less expensive than cars,
they are fast, and
they are noisy.

7. Review infinitives, participles, and gerunds. Give students a verb. Ask one student to use it as an infinitive, another to use it as a participle, and a third to use it as a gerund.

EXAMPLE: yell

Infinitive: The baby likes to yell at two in the morning.
Participle: The yelling six-year-old was dragged out of the circus.
Gerund: Yelling in church is impolite.

EXAMPLE: trot

Infinitive: The horse began to trot through Central Park.
Participle: The horse, trotting briskly, managed to cross the finish line ahead of the Rolls Royce.
Gerund: Trotting may replace jogging as a favorite form of exercise.

120

8. Review combining sentences. Ask one student to provide an interesting first sentence. Ask a second student to provide another sentence, related to the first in content. Ask a third student to combine the two.

EXAMPLE:
(1) Homemade cookies are delicious.
(2) Homemade cookies are inexpensive.
(3) Homemade cookies, though inexpensive, are delicious.

EXAMPLE:
(1) Jock enjoys doing housework.
(2) Jock works out doing weight lifting and push-ups.
(3) Although Jock works out doing weight lifting and push-ups, he also enjoys doing housework.

PORTFOLIO I. SNAKES
Pages 232–241

Have the students read "Put It All Together" on page 232.

To get students into the mood, have them take turns reading aloud the items about snakes on pages 233 and 234. Let them pause frequently to ask questions, to make comments, or just to giggle a little.

1. Finding Answers

Before you begin sentence 1, spend some time discussing the word "relevant."

RELEVANT — that which is logically connected with a particular topic.

Snakes appear on the caduceus, a medical emblem.
Relevant: The snake was once used to treat rheumatism, deafness, and tuberculosis.
Not Relevant: The snake is sometimes 33 feet long.

Emphasize that when the students are writing, only "relevant" material should be included. Ask less able students to give examples:

121

(a) If you are describing the school building, what are some facts that would be relevant? What are some that would *not* be relevant?

(b) If you are writing about a class election, what material would be relevant? What material would not be relevant?

Now have students complete Exercises 1 through 6. Check and discuss.

1. Snakes swallow insects that have been killed by insecticides. The insecticides accumulate in the liver, causing death.

2. $120 to $180

3. 3–5–8–9–10–12–15–17–19–20–21–22–23–24–26–27–30–31

4. 8–27–28–31–33

5. 20–22–32–33

6. 6–7–13–25–26

Since there is a good deal of writing included in each portfolio and since you have limited time for correcting, you may wish to inform the students that after they have completed the portfolio, you will collect their books and grade one of the assignments or correct every assignment.

2. Writing a Report

A few students may need assistance with this essay, but most should be able to complete it successfully if they follow the procedure step by step. Later, have each report read by at least two other students. Have students' comments stapled to each report.

3. Writing a Friendly Letter

After students have completed the friendly letter, check their papers for overall format. Then have several letters read aloud. Encourage discussion not only of the organization and writing, but also of the various points emphasized by different individuals and of the different tones achieved. Emphasize that writing reflects the writer, and let them talk about this curious fact.

4. Writing a Fable

This would be a good time to introduce your students to Aesop's "Fables." Since they are short, you can easily read several, allowing brief discussion after each. Thus fable-fed, students should be able to proceed with this part. Later, have several fables read aloud and discussed. Attach them to the frame of the chalkboard for a few days and encourage students to read some at the beginning and end of the period.

VARIATIONS AND FOLLOW-UPS

1. **Research.** Ask students to divide into four small groups. Then list research jobs:
    (a) Check recent magazine articles about **snakes** in *The Readers' Guide to Periodical Literature*. List at least four articles. Read one article and take notes of any especially interesting material.
    (b) Check articles about **snakes** in at least three encyclopedias. Take brief notes of any especially interesting material.
    (c) Find six quotations about **snakes** (check books of quotations). Note. Check books of world records and fact books for additional information about snakes. Make brief notes.
    (d) Prepare partial bibliography of books about **snakes** available in the school library. Check each book briefly and select the five that look most interesting and most useful. Take notes of some interesting material.

    Have each of the four groups pursue one of the research jobs. Afterward, ask them to share any especially interesting information with the entire class.

2. **Writing.** Challenge students to another page of **snake** items to follow pages 233 and 234. Let each group fill one-half column. Remind them to use their writing skills to make each item as interesting as possible.

PORTFOLIO II. NAMES
Pages 242–251

Have students take turns reading aloud the items about names on pages 242 and 243. Let them pause frequently to ask questions and make comments. Encourage them to add any information they have about names and about how names influence their owners.

5. Writing a Filler

Read and discuss this filler. What other examples are there of discrimination against the Ss and Zs, especially in school? How do the As and Bs feel about it? (They may feel discriminated against too—being called on first, having to occupy the first seats, etc.)

Review the meaning of "relevant."

Have students complete the exercise. Have a few read in class. *Optional.* If you want some or all of your students to have additional practice in writing fillers, consider these titles as possible assignments.

> Unusual Names
> Names of Cars (item 4 in addition to their own knowledge and/ or research)
> How Parents Choose a Name for the Baby (item 15 and research among family members and friends)

6. Writing a Book

Begin this chapter orally, handling parts A and B as a group and allowing students to help each other. Then have them proceed individually. Halfway through J (after students have written a first draft on scrap paper), divide them into small groups and let them read and discuss their first drafts. (Suggestions and ideas may come forth that will help each writer, and comments about vocabulary and sentence structure may help with revisions.)

Have students complete final, polished versions of fillers.

Now—if you like—appoint an editor and an editorial board and turn the papers over to them to use in putting together a class book. All students can be brought into the project from time to time to choose a title for the book, for example, or to help write an introduction.

7. Writing a Friendly Letter

After the students have written friendly letters, have two written on the chalkboard. Ask class members to read and evaluate. Some points that should be considered:

> Is the letter well written? (Consider sentence variety, nouns, verbs, and adjectives.)
> Is there enough material? Is the letter "meaty" rather than just a series of opinions?
> Most important—is the letter persuasive? Would the young parents be persuaded to follow the writer's advice?

8. Writing a Report

Little help should be given in this part. By now, students should be able to apply their knowledge and skill independently. When they have finished their reports, collect and grade.

VARIATIONS AND FOLLOW-UPS

1. **Research.** Have students divide into four small groups. Then list research jobs:
    (a) Check surnames (last names) common in this country to find probable origins. Make notes of interesting ones.
    (b) Develop a long list of celebrities who have changed their names. Include original names and present names.
    (c) Find information about common names (first and last) used in other countries. Pay special attention to China and Sweden. Take notes.
    (d) Develop a list of businesses that have interesting names. (For example, Shear Joy for a hairdressing salon.)

    Have each of the four groups pursue one of the research jobs. Afterward, ask them to share any especially interesting information with the entire class.

2. **Writing.** Ask each group to work together to write a report based on the information found during their research. Remind them to think about the information—to ask "why"—and to draw conclu-

sions. When they have finished, let each group read the reports of the other three.

PORTFOLIO III. MOVIES
Pages 252–260

Have students take turns reading aloud the items about movie special effects on pages 252 and 253. Let them pause frequently to ask questions or to make comments. Encourage them to add any information they have heard about special effects. (Some students may be very knowledgeable in this area, especially about special effects used in the *Star Wars* films.)

9. Writing a Business Letter

Take time to review the format of a business letter. (See page 255 for a sample letter.) Point out the various parts of a business letter: where each is located, how each is punctuated. (Remind students that while there is room for creativity in the composition of a business letter, there is no room for creativity in the format!)

Have students complete the exercise.

If an opaque projector is available, show several letters on a screen and have students read and evaluate by asking the following questions:

> Is the format correct?
> Is the sentence structure good?
> Is the spelling correct?
> Is a mature, forceful vocabulary used?
> Is the paragraphing accurate?
> Is the organization clear and logical?
> Does the letter do the job it was meant to do?

10. Writing a Report

To complete this assignment, students will have to draw on all the writing techniques they have been studying. If you give no help at all, you may wish to use this report as a test. Collect and grade.

11. Writing a Persuasive Letter

Let students work independently. When they have finished, have several letters read aloud and discussed. Emphasize the persuasiveness of each letter.

Optional. A logical follow-up is to have students write a real persuasive letter to the school or the local newspaper. It should concern a personal, school, or community problem and should be written to change the minds of some readers. Encourage the students to send their letters to the school or local newspaper, or let students select a few especially effective ones to submit. The best way to motivate student writing is to help them to see their writing in print—ready to be read by readers other than by a teacher and fellow students. A successful experience of this type will be invaluable and will move students several steps up the writing ladder.

VARIATIONS AND FOLLOW-UPS

1. **Research.** Have students divide into four small groups. Have each group choose one movie or one TV program or special. The movie or TV program must be one that was outstanding, that attracted a good deal of attention, and that is still admired and viewed today.

   Some possible movies:
   Gone With the Wind
   Star Wars
   Jaws
   Sound of Music

   Some possible TV programs and specials:
   Roots
   I Love Lucy
   *M*A*S*H*

Permit students to add to the above lists, but be sure any addition satisfies the three requirements.

   Next, ask each group to find:

1. What is the story (plot or story line)?
2. Were there any problems connected with the filming and how were they solved?

3. How did two reviewers of the movie or program evaluate it?

They should then ask (and answer) these questions:

4. When was the movie or TV program made?
5. What were the mood and interests of this country at that time?
6. Why was this movie or TV program so popular? (based partly on answers to 4 and 5)
7. Why has this movie or TV program continued to be popular? Why is it shown again and again?

2. **Writing.** Finally—ask each group to report on their findings in one well-written article. These should be good enough to be read aloud for the entire class to enjoy.

ANSWERS TO THE UNIT TESTS

The Unit Tests are published in a separate booklet. When ordering please specify: R 438 U or THIRTEEN STEPS TO BETTER WRITING UNIT TESTS.

Unit Test One

PART I. TESTING YOUR MEMORY

I. 1. a word that names a person, place, or thing
    2. a word that expresses action or the state of being
    3. a word that describes a noun
    4. a general statement
    5. a word that means the same or almost the same as another word

II. 1. body of water; ocean; Atlantic
    2. land mass; continent; North America
    3. animal; dog; Doberman
    4. food; vegetable; peas
    5. vehicle; car; Dodge

III. (Answers will vary.)

    1. eat—swallow—gulp
    2. walk—amble—strut
    3. talk—chat—yammer
    4. hit—strike—smash
    5. say—declare—insist

IV. (Answers will vary.)

    1. a round, red apple
    2. a sleek, shining car
    3. a dreary, dirty street
    4. a tiny, tangerine bird
    5. a monstrous, mumbling dinosaur

V. 1. g   6. h
    2. f   7. c
    3. b   8. e
    4. j   9. a
    5. i   10. d

PART II. TESTING YOUR WRITING

I.   (Answers may vary.)

1. unhappy
2. a little
3. a lot
4. one thrifty housewife
5. battered
6. $3000
7. A socialite
8. tossed
9. mink
10. the white elephant
11. picked up—discovered
12. proclaiming
13. disappeared
14. her treasure
15. an absent-minded woman
16. hidden
17. diamonds
18. begging
19. unintentioned bonanzas
20. saying

II.   (Answers will vary.)

Unit Test Two

PART I. TESTING YOUR MEMORY

I.   1. a word that describes a verb, adjective, or other adverb
      2. a word that takes the place of a noun
      3. a word that shows relationship
      4. the result of correcting and improving a piece of writing
      5. the point (or person) from which a story is viewed

II.   (Answers will vary.)

1. skillfully
2. Painfully
3. competently

4. frequently
5. never

III.   1. it's; its
      2. They're; their
      3. You're; your
      4. I; her
      5. We; our

IV.   (Answers may vary somewhat.)

      1. at; to
      2. of; for; of
      3. in; with
      4. among; with; as

V.   1. According to time: from the earliest event to the latest.
        (Answers will vary.)
     2. According to space: from top to bottom; from left to right.
        (Answers will vary.)

PART II. TESTING YOUR WRITING

I.   (Answers may vary.)

1. insisted		14. annual
2. incredible		15. powerful
3. informed		16. tossed
4. to		17. from
5. exactly		18. occasion
6. fascinating		19. amazing
7. into		20. competing
8. Perhaps		21. fiercely
9. used		22. with
10. unusual		23. object
11. thoughtfully		24. gives
12. him		25. on
13. enthusiastic		

II.   (Answers will vary.)

131

Unit Test Three

PART I. TESTING YOUR MEMORY

I.   1. A sentence that makes a statement.
       2. A sentence that asks a question.
       3. A sentence that gives a command.
       4. A sentence that shows surprise or shock.
       5. A question that is not meant to be answered, that the speaker or writer intends to answer.

II.   (Answers may vary somewhat.)

       1. How fast does a baby giraffe grow?
       2. My name is _____ .
       3. Stay away from skunks.
       4. Help me, somebody!
       5. Why should *you* eat Abominable Snowman cereal?

III.   1. Fireflies give light, but it would take more than 228,000 fireflies to equal the light given by a 100-watt light bulb.
       2. Will you catch 228,000 fireflies, or will Jason?
       3. A firefly is male, and a glowworm is female.
       4. Millions of glowworms live in some caves in New Zealand, and their lights, playing on the rock formations, create a fairyland atmosphere.
       5. The firefly has wings; the female firefly, the glowworm, is wingless.

IV.   1. Edmond Rostand wrote *Cyrano de Bergerac* while sitting in his bathtub because only there was he safe from interruptions.
       2. Although you can't take a cold bath on Sunday in Teruel, Spain, you can take a hot one.
       3. If all the water cascading over Niagara Falls went into bathtubs, it would fill 240,000 tubs every minute.
       4. A brush salesman was arrested when he tried to force a woman to sit in her bathtub so he could demonstrate his back-scrubbing brush.

5. After Ben Franklin brought a slipper bath back from France, he spent hours sitting in it and reading.

V. 1. A compound sentence is made up of two independent clauses connected by a coordinate conjunction. A complex sentence is made up of an independent clause and a dependent clause connected by a subordinate conjunction.
2. A "tour de force" is an act of strength, skill, or ingenuity.
3. and—cc   although—sc
   because—sc   but—cc
   since—sc
4. A paragraph organized chronologically is organized according to time: from the earliest event to the latest. A paragraph organized spatially is organized according to space: clockwise or counterclockwise, for example. A paragraph organized categorically is organized according to categories or classes of people, places, or things.

PART II. TESTING YOUR WRITING

I.   (Answers may vary.)

1. declares	14. with
2. and	15. while
3. of	16. dreamed up
4. enthusiastically	17. even
5. him	18. current
6. working	19. swinging
7. and	20. while
8. for	21. suggest
9. Since	22. meaningfully
10. its	23. general
11. booming	24. in
12. In	25. his
13. made	

II. (Answers will vary.)

Unit Test Four

PART I. TESTING YOUR MEMORY

I. 1. A phrase that describes, identifies, or defines the noun or pronoun it follows.
    2. The parallel parts of a sentence must be similar in structure.
    3. A verbal formed by combining "to" with a verb.
    4. A verbal formed by adding "–ing" or "–ed" to a verb which is then used as an adjective.
    5. A verbal formed by adding "–ing" to a verb which is then used as a noun.

II. 1. A pair of false eyelashes owned by Joan Crawford, the famous movie star, sold for $800 at an auction.
    2. David Martin, a traveler who was annoyed by the dirty drinking glasses in many hotels, invented a paper cup—and became a millionaire.
    3. To raise measuring instruments 60 miles high, weatherpersons use a rockoon, an instrument half rocket and half balloon.
    4. Popcorn, a favorite snack today, was already popular 56,000 years ago.
    5. The name "Muppets," a combination of "puppet" and "marionette," was created by Jim Henson and Joan Nebel, a husband and wife team.

III. 1. The principal deserts in the world include the Sahara and Libyan deserts in North Africa, the Arabian, and the Gobi desert in central Asia.
    2. From a 1,000-pound steer, you get 450 pounds of meat, marshmallows, soap, and violin strings.
    3. Federal payroll checks are stored for seven years, then recycled into bathroom tissue, and used in the restrooms of Federal buildings.
    4. The mood of the average worker is good when he starts the day, slips a little at 11:00 A.M., picks up at lunchtime, and plunges sharply at 3:30 P.M.

134

5. Among the most interesting hotdogs are the Chihuahua, which is doused with chili sauce, the Dachshund which is covered with sauerkraut, and the Poodle, which is served with onions.

IV. 1. To set a world record, Bennett D'Angelo in 1977 ate three pounds and six ounces of ice cream in ninety seconds.
2. Measuring just 19 5/16 inches in width, the narrowest street in the world, in Port Isaac, England, is "Squeeze-Belly Alley."
3. Delivering a 72-hour sermon in 1977 made the Reverend Tony Leyva of West Palm Beach, Florida, the holder of the record for the longest sermon.
4. The longest word in the Oxford English Dictionary is flocciparicinihilipilification, meaning "the action of estimating as worthless."
5. To engineer the longest recorded tow in history, Frank Elliott and George Scott of Nova Scotia in 1927 persuaded 168 motorists to tow their engineless Model T Ford a distance of 4,759 miles.

V. 1. by combining into a compound sentence
2. by combining into a complex sentence
3. by turning one sentence into an infinitive phrase
4. by turning one sentence into a participial phrase
5. by turning one sentence into a gerund phrase
6. by turning one sentence into an appositive
7. by using parallel structure

PART II. TESTING YOUR WRITING

I. (Answers will vary.)

II. (Answers will vary.)